GOD'S MOVING SPIRIT

Series editor:
Professor Geoffrey Lampe, D.D.
Regius Professor of Divinity, University of
Cambridge

GOD'S MOVING SPIRIT

THE CHURCH NOW AND THE CHURCH TO COME

by

T. Ralph Morton

MOWBRAYS LONDON & OXFORD

© 1973 by T. Ralph Morton

Printed in Great Britain at
The Pitman Press, Bath

ISBN 0 264 64614 2

First published 1973
by A. R. Mowbray & Co Ltd
The Alden Press, Osney Mead
Oxford, OX2 0EG

To Jenny with Love

ACKNOWLEDGEMENTS

I should like to express my indebtedness to Ron Beasley, Mark Gibbs, Norman Motley, Roger Sawtell, Gordon Strachan, Brother Thomas of Taizé, Catherine Widdicombe, George Wilkie and very specially to John Casteel and Brian Frost. They are not likely to agree with all the opinions I have expressed, but without their help my opinions would have lacked substance. My thanks are also due to Richard Mulkern for his initial suggestion and his help thereafter.

I would also thank the Editor of 'Community' for permission to quote from Andrew Rigby's article; the SPCK for permission to quote from *America is Hard to Find* by Daniel Berrigan; the Saint Andrew Press for the quotations from *God outside the Church* by J. W. Stevenson: Messrs Hodder and Stoughton for permission to quote from *Mankind my Church* by Colin Morris.

Contents

1   *Has the church a future?*

CAN THE CHURCH survive? Prophets in plenty say it can't. Its critics—and in number they far exceed the prophets—say that it is out-of-date in organisation, un-intelligible in theology and irrelevant in action; that it makes a rapidly lessening impact on the young; that it belongs to the middle-aged who will soon be senile and to the middle classes whose day is done. And few would say that they are entirely wrong. But he would be a rash man who would fix an early date for the demise of the Church. In twenty years? fifty years? a hundred years? All down its history the Church has shown an extraordinary ability to survive. A much more frightening and perhaps as likely a prospect is that in twenty, fifty or even a hundred years it will be much the same as it is now.

But, indeed, its unaltered survival is as unlikely as its total extinction. Events will see to that. Radical change in the Church's life is inevitable and is independent of its attitude to change. Change may be forced on the Church by economic revolution in which the financial fabric of the Church could collapse. It is more probable that change will come more slowly and more certainly through alteration in the way in which men and women work and the way their families live and the way national and international life is organised. Change will come through new freedoms made available by education and increased economic power, and through the sharing of life with those of other beliefs and opinions. The Church's ability to survive will not depend on its stubborn resistance to change, even if a certain stubborn blindness is sometimes a help to survival. Its continuing existence will depend on its willingness and ability to adapt to new conditions. But there will be frustration unless there are now some people making new experiments and others interested enough to learn from them. The future is unpredictable. But what the Church may become in changed circumstances depends on what its members, or at least some of them, are trying to do in present circumstances. In other words it depends on its willingness to be moved by the wind of the spirit.

And things are happening. Some people are so appalled at the prospect of the Church never changing, but only getting smaller and weaker and more ineffective, that they are prepared to do something themselves. Some, not so desperate, want to try new ways to revive old patterns. Others are not interested in such experiments within the institutions of the Church. They are trying to find a significant and satisfying way of life for themselves. They are not making an experiment to see if something works. They are doing something because they do not see anything else for them to do. It is not the prospect of the Church slipping into a twilight existence that moves them, but the determination not to slip into a twilight existence themselves. Of course all these people feel dissatisfaction and exasperation and even despair as they look at the Church as they know it. But despair is not their motive. Indeed no one can take any kind of creative action without knowing something of vision and joy, intention and hope.

So there are multitudes of enterprises which may be pointers to the form of the Church of the future. There are too many even to count, for some are hidden and even secret while others are public and visible. But they are all broadly of the two types already mentioned. There are the endeavours of groups to find for themselves a contemporary pattern of christian living. And there are the experiments which the Church, at some level of its authority, initiates after careful study and often with hesitation. For the leaders of the Church know that new ways must be found and yet they are apprehensive of failure. When the Church today tries to face the challenge of change and adjustment it looks back to the past and finds warning as much as encouragement. For change has rarely brought peace to the Church. And peace is something that it has always valued, perhaps overvalued.

The greatest experiment in radical change made by the Church in the past was the Reformation (including the Counter-Reformation). It was preceded by many strange experiments and it broke the Church. No one likes the word now, except those who think that nothing worth doing has happened since. Only some theologians talk as if a new Reformation was either desirable or possible. And they too put a question-mark over it, as John Robinson did with his book *The New Reformation?* As he says, Vatican II marked the end of the Counter-Reformation. And many would add that the Protestant Reformation had already lost its significance for the modern world. However radical are the changes men want to see, the word 'Reformation' is for us now more of a warning than an example. It harps too much on the past. Its painful associations are with the imposition of belief, intolerance and the creation of division.

The Church has found it safer to talk about Renewal. The word is a useful compromise. It combines the attraction of the new with the conservation of the old. And it recalls respectable examples in the past: the religious orders of Middle Ages, the work of John Wesley, the Oxford Movement of the first half of last century. These were all renewal movements of very different kinds.

Today's renewal projects are apt to be a bit smaller and to be concerned with the life of the parish and the work of the congregation. Sometimes they seem more intent on survival than on discovery. But they are sufficiently realistic to begin with the Church as it is; and hopeful enough to believe the Church capable of change and growth and a new life. They dread the collapse of the Church because they realise the difficulty of ever starting afresh. This is a well founded fear. But fear is not often creative.

These renewal movements are inside the Church. They are seeking to remould its pattern, not to break it. There are other more radical endeavours that deserve the adjective that only a few of them would think of using—'alternative'. They are not trying to renew the face of the Church or to change its form. They are not particularly interested in worship or in organisation. They may hope that what they are doing may have some effect on the Church. But that is not their affair. Their aim is more immediate and more personal. It is either to find a way of life that suits them and those with whom they live, or to enable them to give themselves wholeheartedly, without domination or patronage, to those whom they seek to serve. They want to be free. And so their enterprise or their group becomes for them their place of fellowship, discipline and comfort. It has become for them their alternative to the Church.

These groups are all new. But what they are doing is not new. Nor is their dissatisfaction with the Church. We have had plenty of alternative Churches and alternative movements in the past. Indeed, how did the Church of England come into being but as an alternative Church? Or the Church of Scotland? They were established as alternatives to the old, even if they were both determined to see that in their domains there were to be no other alternatives. And all groups that have broken away from the established order and have set up their own have offered men alternative Churches. Some of these have indeed claimed to be the only one true Church. But not all. There was one that took a more modest name. Two hundred years ago in some parishes in Scotland where a minister was imposed against the wishes of the people, some left and formed what they called a 'relief' Church, as a temporary expedient till things got better and they could go back. This was a real alternative Church. But these 'relief' Churches were not content to remain such. They banded themselves together to form another denomination. But that was the age of secessions and disruptions and alternative denominations.

But there have been other movements which without original intention tended in the end to become in fact alternative Churches. Perhaps their example has more to say to us today. If the eighteenth century was the time for the founding of alternative Churches, the nineteenth was the time for the founding of societies to do things that the Church was not doing. They were lay societies, not ecclesiastical ones. Some were founded to meet the needs of their own members. Others were founded to meet the needs of those for whom the founders felt a deep concern. They claimed unquestioned loyalty to the Church but in a quite definite way they tended to become alternative Churches for those committed to their purposes. This was probably why the Church from the beginning has been rather suspicious of them. There were the missionary societies pledged to the propagation of the Gospel at home and overseas. There were the Bible societies committed to the distribution of the scriptures. There was the YMCA, concerned with the needs of young men, especially those away from home in the expanding cities. There were the student associations having to do with the special intellectual and religious needs of students. Inevitably these societies became for their members the centres where they found company, inspiration and education in the Christian life.

What then is new in the contemporary groups which perhaps with more reason can claim to be alternative churches today? It is not to be found in their dissatisfaction with the Church. For this, though unexpressed, underlay the founding of these earlier societies. Nor is it really to be found in the kind of activities in which they engage. What is new and different is to be found in the climate of their thinking, in their wide variety and in their ephemerality. They are not particularly thinking of their own future. They are not interested in continuity of organisation. They are concerned only with their present moment. They seek freedom from imposed restraints and to be true to what they want to be and to do. If they use the word 'alternative' at all they would use it in reference to society rather than to the Church. They are not so much convinced that the Church is all wrong as that society is all wrong. For them society matters far more than the Church.

At the same time it is strange how their activities are bound up with the idea of a Church. These enterprises are all essentially corporate. Those who form them know that they cannot live as isolated individuals. Their quarrel with society is that they feel condemned to do so. In protest they feel that they must get together with other people. They must find the significance of their own lives in the significance of the life that they live with other people. However intensely they may feel that the Church has failed them, they know that they cannot exist without something similar to what they know the Church ought to be. And in a quite remarkable way they use the name of Jesus. If we are seriously worried about the possible forms of life for the Church in the future, we have to understand and perhaps learn from these alternatives.

But why a Church at all? Why should so many rebel

against the Church and still hanker after it? And what in
the end is the Church? Who is included and who excluded?

It is odd that the claim for some form of Christianity
without the Church should not be made more powerfully
today. It would seem to be as plausible and much easier to
comprehend than the plea for Christian faith without belief
in God. There are, of course, those who vocally claim that
they have no need of the Church. Much more eloquent is
the testimony of those who would not think of saying
anything. They have just quietly decided that they do not
need the Church and are acting on that decision. They
would be insulted if it were suggested that they were not
Christians. They would claim to be living christian lives
and indeed to be 'better Christians than a lot of those who
go to church'. They just see no point in the Church. They
see no meaning in its tests of belief, no significance in its
discipline and find no satisfaction in its worship. They form
the largest section of the 'Christian' population of this
country and are well represented in the nominal
membership of the Church. In thinking of the future it
would be foolish to overlook this multitude or to dismiss
their silence as indicating that they have no case.

For a case can be made out for Christianity without a
Church. At least without such a Church as we know
today. An ecclesiastical building is not a necessity for the
Church. The Church of the first two centuries got along
very well without it. The group that meets in the building
and which we have come to identify with the Church is no
more necessary than the building itself. It can be seen as
something that divides off its members from the rest of
mankind just as the building can be seen as a symbol of
exclusion and not of welcome. A recent short but profound
book by W. J. Stevenson is entitled *God outside the
Church.* In it he claims that God is to be known outside the
Church in all the ordinariness of ordinary people doing or-

dinary things. Christian life outside the Church is as
worthy of serious thought. And the idea of mankind as the
body of Christ is a respectable theological idea which has
its roots in the New Testament. It is doubtful whether those
whose testimony is silence would express their views in this
way. But the sense of the unity with other men and women
is undoubtedly present in their silent protest. Clearly they
do not form a church nor would they ever claim to do so.
But as clearly they have found an alternative to the
Church. And it is an alternative chosen by a great many
people. In considering alternative ways of Christian living
we dare not overlook them nor disregard their reasons or
their experience. They may well point to the alternative
Church of the future.

The future of the Church is unpredictable, because the
future of the world is uncertain despite all the books
written about it. What the Church may be like in unknown
circumstances depends on what people are trying to do
now in circumstances which they only partially understand. It is these activities, however weak and ephemeral,
that are pointers to the future. It is these that we must go
on to consider.

As we have already seen, they are of various and widely
different kinds. We can group them a little more
systematically in the order in which we shall consider
them.

There are, first of all, the experiments started some
decades ago deliberately to find the way of life and witness
for the Church in a war-broken world. They were built on
the foundation of the traditions of the past. They saw the
need for the revitalisation of worship, mission and theology
if the Church was to fulfil its mission in a strange new
world. They saw the need for Christians to educate
themselves if they were to act responsibly in the world.
They did not, and still do not, see themselves as in any way

alternative churches but rather as servants of the Church. How effective have they been? Have they had any influence on the Church? What has it been? Have they anything to say about the form of Church life in the future? Have they anything to show about how changes are effected in the Church?

Then there are the attempts of groups to find a significant, satisfying and demanding way of life for themselves. Their emphasis is on living together. Their adopted name is 'commune'. They have their pointed word to say to the Church.

Of another sort are the groups that are brought together because of the common work in which their members are engaged. These groups may be industrial or they may have to do with people in need or be concerned with community development. In such cases membership of the local church may prejudice vital commitment to those with whom work is done or whom they seek to serve. For those so committed their job has become their church.

Then there are the new bodies which gladly take to themselves the title 'Church'. Some see themselves as part of the recognised Church. Others see themselves as quite different but still claim the same, as, for instance, 'The Underground Church'. They are at one in refusing to see the name as the exclusive trade-mark of the historic Churches.

There is, next, the large and amorphous body of those whose alternative is to have no Church.

And—perhaps the most important group of all—there are those who in innumerable congregations are making all manner of experiments and starting all kinds of enterprises, which, in varying degrees of effectiveness, are influencing the way the Church lives and the way in which it will face the future—the great and mixed company of the loyal, the devoted, the hopeful and, perhaps, the satisfied.

We shall need to discuss in more detail these diverse experiments and endeavours. We shall need to try to understand why they have arisen and what they are trying to achieve. We will want to ask questions which those engaged in them might never think of asking. Are they pointers to new forms of Church life in the future? Or are they signs that read 'No thoroughfare'. How easily could they be assimilated into the life of the Church as it exists today? How willing is the Church to change its ways? Are any of these enterprises pointers to the possibility of a quite different kind of Church—a truly alternative Church?

Behind all these questions lies the assumption that some kind of corporate organism is essential for the living of the Christian life. We assume this because it is essential for the living of any kind of human life. And all the experiments and enterprises that we shall be considering make this assumption. For they are all group or corporate activities, even those who seem to want no form.

The field is vast, as wide as the world. Of necessity our survey is very restricted. It is confined to this country with superficial glances at Europe and North America. But all the time we must realise that what may well determine the pattern of the world Church of the future will probably be the enterprises that are now taking place elsewhere in the world, among those less moulded by tradition.

But before we go on to discuss these general and particular topics, we must face two basic questions.

The first concerns the perenniel fact of conflict in the Church. There is the conflict between experiment and conservation, between tradition and the spirit. There is also constant conflict in the Church's attitude to the world: between accommodation and protest. These unending conflicts provide the tensions that keep the Church awake and open to experiment and new endeavour.

The second question concerns the particular nature of

our present situation. We need to understand what are the particular anxieties, questions and hopes that men face today. Otherwise we cannot understand why people do the things they do, why they stay away from the Church, why they want to try new ways for themselves and why they want to build a different kind of society alternative to the present sorry show and why they play with the idea of an alternative Church. What are the factors, sociological, psychological and theological, that make our world so perplexing and exciting and ourselves the strange people we are?

2   *The inevitability of change*

IT IS LIFE that changes. Change is of its nature. Often we're afraid of life. And so we fear change. Change seems to come to us from the outside, to astound and upset. Earthquakes, tornadoes, volcanoes are unpredictable, catastrophic events that change life for many and terminate life for some. But the most significant and lasting changes are made by men themselves. Some are so slow that we do not realise their effects until too late. Others are so rapid that we cannot adjust to them in time. When we talk about living in a time of rapid change we should remember that the changes we know and the changes we fear are all man-made.

The men who have achieved great things in the world and so speeded up the rate of change for others have been those who, generally in youth, have broken away from a familiar background, have explored new territories of experience or have discovered new truths. Ivan Illich has pointed out how this experience of change, welcomed in the past by exceptional individuals, is now the unwelcome lot imposed on all in the West. 'We have ceased to live against a rigid framework. All-enveloping, penetrating change is the fundamental experience of our age, which comes as a shock to those brought up for a different age. In the past the same experience was exceptional and had many appearances: exile, migration, imprisonment, overseas assignment, education, hospitalisation. All these traditionally represent the sudden loss of the environment which has given form to a man's feelings and concepts. This experience of change is now faced as a life-long process by every individual in technological society'.[1]

We as members of the total human race are responsible for the changes and keep alive by reacting to them. We are urged forward by the creative spirit in us and in the world. But as individuals and groups we don't know how to deal with the changes we create. We dither between welcome and resistance. On one side we want life to go on as we have known it. On the other side and at the same time we long for things to be different and to know glory.

Of all human societies and groups none knows this conflict more deeply and painfully than the Church. All human societies know in themselves the conflict between the necessity of holding on to what they value and what they have achieved and the urge to break out into new paths of experience and work. Most families know the conflict in the trivial matter of deciding their next summer holiday—the attraction of the familiar as against the excitement of the new and strange. The Church feels this conflict acutely and can even see it become a matter of doctrinal division, because both points of view are based on deep religious convictions.

There is no doubt that the excitement—or the shock—of the new is the basis of the Christian faith. The life and death and teaching of Jesus had on men the effect of an utterly new and quite inexplicable experiment. It challenged familiar conventions and upset accepted beliefs. It offered to men a future whose symbol was death. Under its light men could turn to the past and find in the unexpected things that had happened to men pointers to the things that Jesus did. But this did not take away from the shock and the surprise and the excitement of the new. The

[1] *The Church, Change and Development* by Ivan Illich (Herder and Herder, New York; 1970); pp. 17, 18

emphasis now was on the new rather than the old, on the future not on the past. And this shock of surprise and the call to a continuing experiment has never quite faded from the Church and has continually been renewed by the spirit of life. It is expressed in the language of the Church—in the shout of praise and in the call to conversion.

But the other attitude, though secondary, is by far the more persistent. And it has its place. We need the familiar to give stability to our lives. We depend on the breath of the spirit to live but we live in the dusty air of common day. We can be only groping seekers of the new. We can only at times catch glimpses of its excitement. If we are to hold on to the new life that we have felt or follow the light that we have glimpsed, we need to take hold of what we have learned and build on it. We dare not let it go. So we use all sorts of means to preserve what we have learned from the past: worship and theology, religious education and tradition. It comes to mean so much to us that we fear anything that challenges it. So we become suspicious of the wind of the spirit and of those who want to try new ways. Of course this conflict is not confined to the Church. Any serious organisation knows it, whether it is political, social or sporting. The constitution, the code of rules, the minutes are seen as safeguarding the aims and the very existence of the organisation. They must not be tampered with. So often they stultify the purposes they seek to serve. The only difference with the Church is that the conflict is much more serious as each line is regarded as of fundamental religious and theological importance.

So in the Church we react to change in two ways. We can see it as threatening what we know we dare not lose. Or we can see it as offering a call to a new obedience. Most of us tend to swing from one side to the other. We want to hold on to tradition for the sake of stability and continuity. At the same time we know that the challenge of Jesus is new every morning. At a period of rapid change some people are keen to welcome any change. Others are more resistant than they would be in gentler circumstances. But history is on the side of change.

As changes come through the actions of men, we need never welcome them as unconditional blessings. We have to learn to use them. And this raises a different conflict for the Church: accommodation versus protest. To live we must come to terms with our environment. To be true to ourselves we may feel we must object.

The Church knows this dilemma, especially when it faces a new or alien situation. It has to translate its faith into the language and life of a quite different experience and tradition. But if it has to adjust itself to a strange new society, it has also to seek to change it. The Church has sometimes failed because it failed to find the proper balance. The Jesuit mission to China in the sixteenth century failed to survive because its representatives became almost entirely assimilated into the life of the Chinese court. The Jesuit mission in Japan a little later took a quite different line. It had no accommodation and was highly successful in making converts. It became so successful and so detached that it was seen as a danger to the state and all its members and followers were killed. To recognise a new situation does not mean that we know how to deal with it.

Today we cannot be unaware of or indifferent to change. The uncomfortable awareness that we live in a rapidly changing world is part of our deliberate thinking and of our subconscious fears. For us as a society in the world today this uncomfortable uneasiness is very like the bewildered feelings of an adolescent youth. He faces the discovery and adoption of an adult world which is to be his own and with it the discovery of himself. We face the discovery of a world that is as strange to us and with it the discovery of ourselves. We share the uneasy self-consciousness of the same situation. But there are great differences. The frustrations of the adolescent arise from his resentful awareness that the adult world comes to him ready-prepared by his elders, that it is not really his and that he has to assert himself to find himself. Our world does not come to us ready-prepared by our forefathers. We do, indeed, inherit a great deal and especially in experience and attitudes. But we do not inherit our most inscrutable problems. They are our own and they are new. The experience of the past cannot help us to solve them. It may, indeed, prevent us from seeing them. But it is only in facing them that we shall find our place and ourselves in our world.

Probably the greatest change that has happened to us in the West is that we no longer live in the security of small detached communities. In the Middle Ages the life of the great majority of people was lived in isolated self-contained communities—the manor, the village, the town, the nation, Christendom. The walls around these communities are all down. Yet we still persist in thinking that they give us the picture of how life should be lived. We feel that we were meant to live in a village and not in a city, in a nation and not in a union of all nations, in Christendom and not in God's world.

And yet in a way we live our life with all kinds of people. We work with them. We live together in the same street. Our children study and play with them at school. And if affluence still assures us of a certain privacy, we are aware that our life depends uncertainly on the labour and poverty of millions of other people. Our inherited structures of church and society do not fit this new cosmopolitan world. We are bewildered. We resent the inevitability of change and the uncharted nature of our daily world and we don't know what to do. We cannot yet take into our imaginations what we acknowledge with our minds, that the world is getting too small for the population we produce and the waste we throw away. But we do know as a fact we cannot escape that the little bit of the earth that we have considered ours is the concern of everyone else and will need to be shared with them.

But our imaginations have accepted the fact of the power that is now in the hands of men. We know that men can do almost anything that they want to do if they are prepared to give it priority over everything else. We cannot avoid knowing that men have walked on the moon. We have the evidence of our eyes. And if men can do this, what can they not do? This gives us a quite new view of the world and of man. The wisdom of the ages—the teaching of the philosophers, saints and sages of the past—told men that they were weak and puny and ignorant, that they were at the mercy of disease and disaster and that life was uncertain and certainly short. Man's original sin was pride—the desire to do what was beyond his knowledge and his power. This view is now out-of-date. And men know it. Man's power and not his weakness is unaccountable. This is a view of man's place in the world that men have never had to face before.

In the 1960's war and the atom bomb were the spectres to frighten men into sanity and peace. In this decade their places have been taken by population and pollution. There are marked differences between the two sets of horrors. One is that whereas one is afraid that nuclear warfare may occur once and once only, population and pollution are going on all the time. But there is another difference that has more effect on ordinary men and women. They see themselves as the victims of war. They have seen the great ones of the earth—emperors, kings, governments, Napoleon, Hitler—as responsible for the tragedies that men have brought upon each other. If they think further and see the cause of tragedy to lie in men's ambition and greed, they still see themselves as the innocent victims. With population and pollution we enter the world of the common man. He realises that it is now in the hands of governments to control the pattern of population. But he is also well aware that in the end population is the affair of ordinary men and women. Nothing about the future population of the world can be achieved without their private co-operation. And, to a lesser degree, the same is true of pollution. Everybody creates waste. The solution of the world's problems of pollution and population can be solved only by the co-operation of its inhabitants. The features of the world that we are beginning to mark out bring this terrifying shift of responsibility from the leaders to the people. But we find it difficult to grasp with our minds.

The features that we have picked out—the open society, power in the hands of men, and a new responsibility—as showing what is new and frightening in our world do not give the full and scholarly picture that the sociologist would give. That has not been the aim. We are trying to understand why some people initiate new experiments and why so many are dissatisfied with present society and the present Church. The people who make the experiments are not often sociologists. An academic study of a problem is often its own reward. Those who are so dissatisfied that they want to start something new are apt to be of a different type. They feel the situation rather than study it. And their feelings make them impatient of the old and set them off blindly searching for something significant and new.

We see the change in people's attitude to the world in the radical change in their sense of fear and of guilt. In previous ages what men feared was the unknown. And there was plenty in man's ignorance to cause fear. Religion made full use of this fear: the fear of hell was the fear of the unknown. Today what men fear is what they know. They fear men's knowledge and what men might do with their knowledge. They even find a certain comfort in the unknown. They are no longer children playing in a world they do not understand and afraid of the dark. They are adults afraid of the responsibility and power put into their hands. They are afraid of the light. We have been trained by generations of teaching to accept the fear of the unknown. We have to learn how to deal with our fear of the known.

A new and untutored responsibility brings with it a new sense of guilt. And guilt can be a debilitating thing. Up to now our guilt has been the guilt of innocence. Our excuse has been that we did not know or we did not realise. Guilt for not doing the things that we know must be done but that men have never done before is a very different thing. Margaret Mead, the eminent American anthropologist, pin-points graphically man's loss of innocence and the powers that he has taken into his own hands when she writes about 'man, struggling over and over again with the loss of innocence and today possessed of powers almost as dread as those refused by Christ in the wilderness.'[1] Guilt can become an excuse; for we feel that there is something moral about feeling guilty and to confess it somehow gets rid of it. But when there is no one else to blame but ourselves—not some other nation, not some other group of men, not even God—guilt takes on another face—our own. This guilt is something that we in the West cannot transfer to any one else. To the rest of the world we are 'the powers that be' responsible for their condition. We may try to wriggle out of our responsibility. We may claim that we have no power because we do not know what to do. But this is only the measure of our guilt. We are afraid to do what we know we can do.

[1] *Man in Community: Christian Concern for the Human in Changing Society* edited by Egbert de Vries (S.C.M. Press, 1966). Quoted from *Cultural Man* by Margaret Mead, p. 217.

In this morass of fear and guilt and of hope because of the new possibilities open to men, men are looking for something that will satisfy their hearts and minds. They are looking for some company where they can feel that they personally belong. It has to be clear and simple enough to carry its own authenticity. It must not bear the trade-mark of someone else. It cannot be accepted on someone else's authority. For authority is suspect. This is due not so much to disillusionment with advertisement and propaganda as to the feeling that the authorities to whom appeal is made belong to a world that has passed away.

These changes in our experience and in our picture of the world affect the way we think about the Christian faith. Inevitably our thinking today is confused. The things of which we cannot help thinking are strange and new and real. And these things are the material in which alone we can think about God. And because we are confused by reality, we are beginning to be able to think theologically. This is true of those who scorn the old, familiar religious words and reject even the word 'God'.

It is not a lack of seriousness that leads to this rejection. Events and our experience of the world have broken down walls that we had taken too much for granted. Indeed we built much of our religious life and our theology on divisions. Our divisions expressed our faith: the divisions between spirit and matter, heaven and earth, Church and world, soul and body and the divisions between the denominations. Now we see that we can make no claim on God. He belongs to all men. We dare not in Jesus' name make divisions between good men and bad, Christian and non-Christian. He is the first-born of every creature. We can no longer talk about the Church being on the defensive or on the attack. We come back to all men, and to Jesus.

It's not surprising that many men and women want to find a more adequate way of life for themselves. It's not

surprising that many loyal members of the Church are
convinced that they must find new ways for the Church, if
they are to live as they know they ought to be living. It's
not surprising that some others leave the Church in
despair. It's not surprising that some few want to make
some new effort on their own. It's not even surprising that
some become interested in the experience of those of other
traditions and turn to the East to learn the ways of
mysticism and contemplation.

What would be surprising would be if men and women
were not doing these things.

3   *Signs of renewal*

ALL OVER THE world men and women are trying new
ways of doing things, or looking for new ways or being
forced to adopt new ways. They know that life is changing
and that they are being made to change too. They feel
bewildered or expectant. This need to find new ways and
this urge to seek new ways are seen in education, in industry, in politics and in the Church. Perhaps of all institutions the Church is the most uncomfortably sensitive
to the situation. It knows the need of change. It also knows
the cost of change. For the Church has always known that
in its treasures are things both new and old. And if in Jesus'
words and teaching the new has the priority, the old often
seems to have the greater appeal for conservation. What
inspires men everywhere to find new ways is, for the
Church, the spirit it knows as the breath of its life, creative,
disturbing, revealing, uniting.

So it is not surprising that men and women, made uncomfortable both by their situation and by their faith,
should want to try something new on their own or in the
Church. Some of these experiments are independent and
spontaneous. Others are engineered. Some may be very
odd but all are personal. Many of them come to nothing.
Most, in their present form, will pass away. But they are
evidence of the frustrations, convictions and longings of
men and women. They show how some want to live in the
present. They are also pointers—perhaps the only pointers
we have—to the kind of life Christians may want to live in
the future.

It is of some of these endeavours that we want to think.

22

They arise out of very different situations. They are intent on different aims—the finding of a more personal form of social living, or the nature of work, or the care of others, or the form of the Church itself. They are, therefore, not related to each other, often unorganised and sometimes rather hidden. But before we consider them more fully we should think of the experiments that were initiated earlier, at the time of or immediately after the Second World War. They were rather different. They were related to the Church and often to each other. They were conspicuous and wanted to be so. They were, in this sense, public rather than private. But they set the scene for the very different experiments that many now feel they have to make. Indeed they may be said to have helped to inspire them by giving new ideas and instilling the possibility of change, by training people to do things for themselves and, perhaps, through disappointment at their lack of effectiveness. They are important, also, because they illustrate how experiments can be made, how the Church makes use of them or reacts to them, either by learning or by repudiation. And, as we consider them with the partial detachment of two decades of history, we may well ask ourselves how we assess results. Is the success of an experiment to be seen in the interest and even approbation of outsiders? Or by the adoption of its methods by others? Or in the satisfaction, joy and enlightenment that have come in the doing to those who took part?

The post-war decade was a time of great experiment in the Church. There were almost certainly then more small experiments, of self-appointed groups or of Church-directed action, than there are today. These were the expression of men's ardent hopes at the end of the war, of their sense of the need for reconstruction and of a naïve expectation that all things were now possible. Many of these have passed into oblivion, having achieved their pur-

poses or failed in them. Others there were that succeeded
so well that they have become accepted institutions. In
1956 the newly constituted World Council of Churches
published a booklet that described some of these. It was
called *Signs of Renewal* and described the attempts that
were being made to find new ways towards the recovery of
Christian life in Europe. It was not with the renewal of
Church structures that these experiments were concerned,
but with the renewal of society. They were all concerned
with awakening people generally and Christian people in
particular to a sense of their responsibility for their community, their nation and the world. Their interest lay in the
lay, secular life of the members of the Church rather than
in the religious and ecclesiastical life of its institutions.
Some of the movements welcomed in the booklet as signs
of renewal had been started before the war. Indeed Sigtuna
in Sweden had come into existence at the time of the First
World War. But it was the tragedy of war and the con-
sequent need to rebuild a new nation, a new Europe and a
new world that inspired most of these enterprises. They
were united in a concern for the laity. And indeed it was at
this time that the word 'laity' came into fashion.

Conspicuous among them were the Evangelical
Academies of Germany, called into being to help the laity
to take a new and responsible place in the new life of Germany. There were the Lay Institutes of the Netherlands
and of Switzerland and houses in France, Sweden and
Finland, Agape in Italy, William Temple College at Rugby
and others.

These were all signs because they were visible. They had
houses that man could visit and live in and where they
could meet other people. They were signs because they
spoke of familiar things. They encouraged people to talk
about their daily jobs and ordinary lives. They gave men's
anxieties and hopes a new relevance and a new challenge.

They were signs because they were seen to be building something new after the destruction of war. They were signs of renewal because, like Coventry Cathedral, they were built out of the destruction of the old, to rebuild the old in a new form.

They were not directly trying to find new patterns for the life of the Church. They were not trying to live a life of their own. They saw themselves as fulfilling certain limited purposes, mainly of an educational nature. They trusted that these would be of value to the Church but they were pursued for their own sakes. They were seeking to help particular groups of people to fit themselves for what they were doing or should be doing in the world. They certainly had no intention of becoming alternative Churches.

But there were some movements that set out deliberately to affect the total life of the Church. As a sign of their intention they adopted the word 'community'. It was no new word. In the inter-war years it had been adopted by new societies of committed devotion and service such as the Community of the Resurrection. Such communities, with others like The Society of the Sacred Mission, the Society of Saint Francis in England and the Little Brothers and Sisters of Jesus on the Continent, were founded on the belief that a full corporate life was needed to maintain their devotion and service. They saw community as an absolute need in the Christian life and as a necessary instrument in Christian service. The post-war communities of which we are thinking used the word with a wider meaning. Their members were indeed seeking the same sense of community within their own fellowship. But they were as much concerned with the need of community in society and in the world. They sought not so much to rebuild community in the Church as to help men to rediscover community in a strange, new world. And their appeal to men lay in this.

We take two of these new communities for fuller

study—The Community of Taizé and the Iona Community. They cannot be taken as typical of anything but
themselves. But, then, any new enterprise or experiment is
unique. The Iona Community is included in *Signs of
Renewal*; Taizé is not. This exclusion is not due to any late
foundation of Taizé. Indeed Taizé had its first small beginning during the last war, while Iona was started just before
the war. But Iona was seen from the beginning as having to
do with lay people, while Taizé was only to reveal this interest later. These two communities have many similarities
but their differences are more marked.

They both adopted the name 'community'. Each took as
its home a place of historic religious association—Iona
and Cluny. Both were powerfully moulded by the past:
Iona by going back to Columba and the Celtic Church,
and taking the completion of the restoration of a ruined
Benedictine abbey as their practical work. The Community
of Taizé by following the monastic discipline of the
religious life but in a quite new way. Both belong to the
Presbyterian or Reformed tradition. Both, in different
ways, have seen their work as ecumenical. Both have been
committed to the revitalisation of worship. Both have
stressed Christian responsibility in politics, especially in action for the poor of the world. By all these means they have
attracted to themselves curiosity and suspicion, while at
the same time they have given hope to many.

These similarities might suggest that both communities
belong to the past. Their differences offer more significant
pointers to the future.

The Community of Taizé is a 'religious' brotherhood in
the strict sense of the word 'religious'. It is composed of
some seventy-five men who have bound themselves
together by what they prefer to call 'engagements' rather
than vows: to give up private property, to be celibate and
to obey the discipline and direction of the order. Taizé

became a reality in the mind of Roger Schutz, its prior, during the war and from then has never ceased to develop. It thus came into being in France when society was broken, the Church confused and men not knowing where to turn for hope. Men who felt called to a life of devotion and service felt that, if they were to do anything, they needed something more sustaining, more comforting and more demanding than the individualistic life of the Reformed Church. A religious order can do work that individuals cannot do by themselves. This is because of their corporate discipline, undistracted by family commitments, and because of the wide variety of abilities and skills among their members, and also because of assured continuity.

And the Community of Taizé has done remarkable work along many lines. It has pioneered agricultural development in its neighbourhood and undertaken medical work. It has developed crafts, especially pottery, and set up a printing press. The works of scholarship which its members have produced are outstanding. It has sent out brothers to serve all manner of social, political and ecumenical causes all over the world, particularly among the poor, as, for instance, in South America. It has in the past probably been best known for the leading part it has taken in dialogue with the Roman Catholic Church.

It has always seen its work in terms of reconciliation. The composition of its membership has pointed to the breaking down of national barriers. Its home is in France. Its founder is Swiss. Its members come from France, Switzerland, the Netherlands, Germany, Britain and other countries. They belong to many denominations and the clerical members are ordained by their home Churches. It is thus a symbol of unity—the unity of the Church and the unity of the world. In its ecumenical membership and in its close contact and co-operation with the Roman Catholic

Church, the Church of England and other Churches of differing traditions from its own, the Community certainly offers a pointer to the world Church of the future. But if this ecclesiastical interest was all, would youth be interested?

For young people are undoubtedly interested and the Community's interest is at the moment in youth.

Youth had early found a welcome at Taizé. There was nothing enclosed about the life of its community. Visitors were not shut out from the life of the brothers. Young people were attracted by the sight of a company of men living a happy life without personal property and in the service of others, and especially by the surprising fact that they could share this life while they were there. The community has seen this openness as part of their life. The simplicity of their style of living reinforces this openness. There is no great refectory where the members eat together. Their life is organised in little groups like families, and in these visitors feel at home.

The influx of youth led to the acceptance of an obligation to youth, an obligation to let young people use them. In 1972 between January and September 60,000 young people stayed at Taizé. Out of their numbers and their interest has come the decision to hold a Council of Youth, something on the lines of the Councils of the early Church or of Vatican II but a Council *of* Youth not *for* youth. It is on this that the life of the Community now seems to be focussed. The Council is seen as something that has already begun, in the questions and the hopes and the frustration of young people. To quote their leaflet on it: 'The Council cannot be just a discussion, or some organised group: it will be what it already is—a search for a worldwide communion in our diversity, a style of life in contradiction with received values of self-seeking, domination, careerism; it will be attentive to those who are poorest.' The Council will meet in 1974 but it 'will last several years—time to include many ways of living this, in every part of the world.' Already preparation is going on in cells in many countries. But 'the preparation of the Council is to be lived more than thought-about or talked about.' The Council is open to all, Christians and non-Christians alike, and especially to those from the poorer world.

Is this a picture of the Church of the future? Who can say? Youth assembled at Taizé at Easter, 1970 declared that they saw the risen Christ 'preparing for us a springtime of the Church—a Church devoid of the means of power, ready to share with all men, a place of visible communion for the whole of humanity.'

But nagging questions remain.

If this is a picture of the Church of the future, what happens to the Church as we know it? Do we just write it off and start afresh?

It is not difficult to foresee the rise of groups, similar to the Community of Taizé or linked to it, dedicated to the service of men and the mission of the Church. And with them the work of the Church would be done with great efficiency and reliable continuity. But staff and shock troops, even if numbered in thousands, do they make up humanity or the Church?

And what happens when the young in their thousands become middle-aged with jobs to maintain, and families to rear and political responsibilities personally to fulfil and the burden of the world to carry?

Such questions haunt all new experiments. The Iona Community faces different questions but as difficult.

The Iona Community is not a 'religious' community in the sense in which the Community of Taizé is. It is a fellowship of men and, now, some women (in all, 130 members) who share a common discipline, renewed each year, but who have not given up their responsibilities in

jobs, families or in social and political life. Indeed the purpose of the Iona Community is to help its members to be
responsible in their secular life and through them hopefully
to help members of the Church generally. So members of
the Iona Community do not go out to work in the name or
at the direction of the Community; except those on its staff.
Their position as parish ministers, or workers in industry,
or teachers or doctors or social workers is exactly the same
as that of other people in similar jobs. What the Community offers them is a society in which they are free to discuss
all the questions that arise in their life with those who share
their basic convictions and the same initial training.

Their training is only for a short period on Iona. The rest
is on their job out in the world. Those who join spend their
first three months living and working and worshipping
together in the Abbey on Iona. For the first thirty years of
the Community's life this experience was centred on the
manual work of completing the restoration of the ruined
mediaeval buildings. The demands of construction—of
stone and wood, of weather and the stage of the work—
determined their life for the summer. During these months
the craftsmen members were the teachers and the ministers
the apprentices. This co-operation of clergy and laity on a
secular job was vital to the growth of the Iona Community.
Men were learning to work together and, perhaps, to understand each other in their different jobs. Now that the
work of building is at an end, new members still have this
initial period on Iona but its temper has changed. No
longer does the job to be done determine the pattern of life.
Now the determining factors are the concerns of the
members. Life on Iona has ceased to be life on a building
site. It has become more like life in a mixed and constantly
changing congregation. But this may, indeed, bring the
Iona Community a stage further on in its purpose.

The avowed purpose of the Iona Community was to find

new ways of life and witness for the Church in a new age. It was founded by George MacLeod the year before war broke out. It arose out of the extreme economic depression and unemployment on the Clyde in the 1930's. It was thus the industrial situation that brought the Iona Community into existence. It arose out of the desperate situation in which the unemployed were placed and the failure of the Church to deal with their plight. It was this that determined that the Community should be made up of young ministers and craftsmen, and that led George MacLeod to adopt the task of completing the rebuilding of the Abbey on Iona as the continuing work on which all were to begin their training. It was into the industrial areas of greatest suffering that they were sent to complete it. The concern of the Iona Community was with the situation men were in. War which came so quickly only revealed the size of the problem of an industrialised world. It was on this that the eyes of the Community were set. It was this concern with the life of men in the world that made the Community early adopt as a rule that they should not have for themselves any scheme of discipline or way of living that could not be carried out in a parish. The fact that the laymen members of the Community—now of many occupations and professions—are in ordinary secular jobs and the ministers engaged mainly in ordinary parish work has meant that the feet of the members of the Community have been almost too solidly on the muddy ground of an industrial society. This has kept its discussion of the work of its members down to earth and suspicious of lofty theories. It has kept its high flying to political protests and demands.

As with Taizé, the primary appeal of the Iona Community, especially in the first two decades of its life, lay in the sight of a group of men living a corporate life, in a romantic setting indeed, but engaged in an ordinary job of work. This appeal was reinforced by the chance of joining in the life and sharing in the work. Men desperately seeking for some creative action in their own lives found significance in this enterprise, especially when its members had not opted out of ordinary life but faced all its uncertainties in the cities for most of the year. The Community was open: open to visitors, open in its worship, open in its conferences; open to young people who from the beginning insisted on coming and for whom camps have now been run for many years. Here the purpose is not so much to bring them together on Iona as to get them concerned with what they do when they go back to the industrial areas where they live and work. For this reason the contemporary interest of the Community is in unemployed youth.

The second appeal of the Iona Community has been its interest in the ordinary life of lay people. This interest was present from the beginning, but it has developed with the years through increased understanding of the secular nature of the world's problems and the realisation of the failure of the Church to do anything significant about them: we all have to educate ourselves in the business of living together with all other men in the world today. The Iona Community now includes in its membership a fair number of members in positions of some responsibility in their professions and in society who bring a very varied an articulate contribution to discussion and understanding.

What effect has the Iona Community had on the life and work of the Church? It has without doubt influenced the Church of Scotland in many ways: in the promotion of parish mission, in worship, in the ministry of healing and in a general opening up of discussion and action on political issues. Through its own industrial work it certainly led the Church of Scotland to undertake industrial mission and probably influenced its recent advocacy of political responsibility and action on the part of its members. This widening of the area of things discussed and things done represents a more vital change in the life of the Church than any organisational reform. The greatest contribution of the Iona Community has probably been to give some people confidence to think and to act.

Neither Taizé nor Iona have seen themselves as alternative churches. They have rather seen themselves as helping the Church as a whole to find wider areas of action and witness, a deeper devotion and greater skills. And, of course, there are many other enterprises with the same aims. Some of them have already been mentioned as being in the original booklet *Signs of Renewal*. All of them were equally intent on widening this area of concern and on helping men to greater responsibility in political action. A few of those mentioned in the booklet have vanished. Others have taken their place. In Britain there are, for instance, Lee Abbey, which claims to be 'now the largest mixed religious community in Europe', Scottish Churches House at Dunblane, the only organisationally ecumenical house in Britain, Scargil in Yorkshire, Dartmouth House in South London, Carberry in Scotland. These have the avowed aim of serving the Church by bringing people together for study and discussion. They are residential and know the value of sharing ordinary life and worship even if only for a very short time. They depend on the vision and endurance of the staff which is always too small. They lack the support of a wider community, engaged in other tasks than the affairs of the house and committed to working out new ideas in action and not only in words.

The Community of Taizé and the Iona Community are marked off from these smaller societies by their large and continuing membership engaged in a multiplicity of jobs in many places throughout the world. It is this and the welcome they offer to all sorts of people that have made them visible tokens of hope for many. To many of those trying today to find more radical ways they may seem strangely devoted to traditional worship and mediaeval discipline and too involved in ecclesiastical affairs. But what these two historic communities have given to men, each in its own way, has been significant and basically the same. First of all, and perhaps most important, they have given to men infectious evidence of the possibility of men living and working together in community and continuing to do so. Secondly, their welcome to others and their acceptance of them as they are and not as they think they should be has been a surprising revelation of the openness of the Christian life. Thirdly, because of their concern with the ordinary daily life and work of men they have brought to men the comfort of knowing that their labours are of importance. And lastly, and as an irritant to many, they have protested the need of a positive and even a rebellious line in political affairs—for the poor of the world.

The experiments we go on to consider have carried these ideas further. But perhaps without the witness of these older, stable communities some would not have had the nerve to move at all. Even the feelings of frustration they have engendered in some may have been what inspired them to new action and therefore the new hope. Continuity may be needed to give a lasting background to sporadic experiments.

4   *Communes*

IN THE WEST there is today among many people, especially those who are young, an almost overpowering urge to find a way of living with others of a like mind on their own terms and in their own style. It springs from despair and even from disgust, but also from hope. It leads to experiments very different from those we have been considering. These were organised and recognised, often identified with an outstanding personality as founder and claiming a place in society by holding property, making plans and having a constitution. What we find today is a rash of small groups, under many names, with diverse purposes, anonymous, unorganised, ephemeral. They talk the old language of community but prefer the more politically loaded word 'commune' to emphasise their difference.

The great difficulty in discussing them is that there are too many to count, too varied to allow generalisations and too ephemeral to permit accuracy. Most would repudiate their right or their desire to use the adjective 'christian'. Even those who might well use it would not all want to. An informed observer reports that in Edinburgh there are to his knowledge, and at the time, some five groups that could perhaps claim both the words 'commune' and 'christian'. And this number would seem to be fairly typical of the country as a whole.

A sociologist has this to say: 'It is very difficult to estimate the actual numbers of such experiments. In 1969 I read a report which estimated that there were over five hundred communal ventures with a total membership of over ten thousand in the United States. In Japan it has been estimated that there are some fifty communes and approximately three hundred co-operative villages. On the continent of Europe communes have sprung up in most of the major cities, inspired to some extent by the example of the Kommune which was founded by some young radicals in Berlin in March 1967, whose members received a great deal of publicity as a consequence of their radical activities. In Holland is has been estimated that there are approximately two hundred community ventures run by members of the Roman Catholic Church. In Israel the kibbutz movement has continued to grow to the point where there are some two hundred and thirty-five kibbutzim with a total membership of over ninety thousand—about 4 per cent of the Jewish population in Israel. In Britain I would estimate that there are between fifty and a hundred communes of one sort or another in existence. It is impossible to be more accurate than this in so far as many communes seek to keep their existence as secret as possible in order to avoid the problems that can result from being flooded out with visitors, curious sight-seers and the inquisitive mass media.'

From this survey it appears that the name 'commune' can include widely different groups—economically productive groups, political groups, religious groups. But they all have one thing in common—an economic or at least a sociological interest. They arise out of disillusionment with the established orders of society—the family, the Church, social groups, political parties, industrial organisation. Their members are seeking for themselves a simpler, more authentic, more personally related life.

This contemporary urge has its pattern in the past. The desire to discover a positive and simple way of life is a

[1] 'The Commune Scene in Britain' by Andrew Rigby, in 'Community' No. 3 Summer 1972; pp. 2, 3

recurrent happening in man's history. It can manifestly be traced back to the beginning of Christianity. The Book of Acts and Paul's letters illustrate how the creation of new forms of communal life was the inevitable response to the acceptance of the Gospel. But it goes much further back. It is, indeed, a feature of all religious movements. And it recurs all down the history of the Church. It inspired the foundation of the early monasteries. We see it in the sects that arose in the late Middle Ages and during and after the Reformation. In them were combined protest against the political and economic life of their time and a desire to find the way to a more authentic religious life for themselves. They were all attempts to find a self-contained and self-directed form of social living for a group of like-minded people.

During the last two centuries similar secular communities have arisen. These have been without any avowedly religious foundation though obviously influenced by christian teaching. There were, for example, the experiments in economic community started by Robert Owen at New Lanark in Scotland and in New Harmony in Indiana. Then there have been communities composed of families rather than of individuals.

The most famous and longest lasting of these family communes has been the Brunderhof. It was founded in Germany after the tragedy of the First World War and in the innocent days of the German Youth Movement. It has a definitely religious basis. It is built on a renunciation of private property and on the simplty of family life and daily work. When Hitler came to power it had to leave Germany and settled in England. When war made life in England difficult for a community mainly consisting of Germans, the Bruderhop moved to Paraguay. Now its main centre is in the United States, where it has solved its economic problem by taking over a lucrative toy-making industry. So it has survived fifty years and looks like continuing a quiet life, after many stormy vicissitudes.

But the present movement is no repetition of past experiments, even though they share a similar essential intention, and even though it picks up ideas found in many of the post-war enterprises. All of these expressed the same dissatisfaction with the social and religious life offered to men, the same conviction of the need for some kind of communal life and the same desire to find a simpler way of life. So it is not surprising to find the new magazine *Community* echoing the thoughts of the defunct *Community* magazine of the 1940's. The call to communal life was sounded by many of these earlier movements. For example, the Othona Community, founded in 1946 and still going strong, emphasises simplicity and, indeed, the austerity of a life based on the family. Agape in Italy emphasised the importance of manual work in bringing people together. These and similar communities valued the continuity provided by a site and a building.

The communes of today do not seek this continuity. They are avowedly personal, limited, spontaneous. And they are ephemeral and are not ashamed to be so. In this they are like the family. A family is not dependent on a house or a location. It is made up of people in a special relationship. It exists only so long as those who form it are there. It exists only for the life that its members live in it. It has not failed when there are no descendents. It can only be personal, spontaneous and ephemeral. Its meaning and its joy depart when it is maintained only for continuity. It may well be that the ephemerality of the commune as we know it today in the West is not so much its weakness as an indication of its significance.

There is little doubt that it is the political implications of the word 'commune' that has led to its adoption. It is also likely that the success of the kibbutz in Israel and of the commune in China has enhanced its popularity. But it is important to remember that there is little similarity between them and the communes we are considering. The kibbutz and the Chinese commune are well established experiments that are indeed economically revolutionary and socially radical. But they are also disciplined units of production with an integral place in the economic system of their country. But the adoption of the name emphasises the basic political and economic interest of the private communes of the West and also their international concern.

Much more influential in example and determinative of pattern have been the communes that arose in America in the 1960's. They arose in protest against the American way of life in general and the Vietnam war in particular. They have been many in number and strange in form. They have not revealed the staying power of the Brunderhof and may well be on their way out. A full study of them is to be found in Richard Fairfield's *Communes USA*. When we turn to Britain we find little so extreme.

We are concerned here with the more sedate forms and more particularly with communes that would not disdain the adjective 'christian'. There are plenty of them as we have seen, even in Britain. They are difficult to list. Some want to remain secret. Others welcome publicity. It is therefore difficult to generalise and dangerous to dogmatise. In this chapter we consider those groups whose prime interest is in communal living. In the next chapter we shall consider groups which come together for the sake of a piece of work or service and which generally would not use the name 'commune'.

These christian groups can be divided into three categories.

There are, first of all, the groups that see themselves and are seen as part of the life of the Church. They are often so respectable that the name 'commune' is almost inappropriate. For all that, they may be the most immediately influencial. Gunnel Valquist, a Swedish Roman Catholic journalist, gives this description of the many such groups she found in Italy; and the description could apply elsewhere. 'The pattern for these dynamic parish groups is almost always the same: at the centre is a fellowship of thirty to forty persons, married and unmarried, often young, sometimes of all ages, living in a kind of communal fashion, to a degree holding all property in common, and seeking to recover the sources of Christianity. They go literally to the Gospel in order to find new and radical patterns of life, and in the Word and Eucharist they seek the way towards an authentic Christian life in both Church and society.'[1] Such groups might be said to be a development of the house groups to be found in many British congregations. These groups are very much part of the local church and can be seen as trying to find a fuller life for a congregation.

The second group is more strictly communal but less directed towards an avowed aim. It is formed of the experiments that groups, often of students, carry out by living together in a house. Very often the experiment is made because of the difficulty of finding ordinary accommodation and the feasibility of joining together to share the expenses of a house of some size. Sometimes a university makes such houses available. Practical necessity and economic convenience are powerful spurs to make such experiments succeed. And sometimes an experiment succeeds better if it is not too self-conscious. Such experiments also gain from the essentially detached life of students and their intellectual concern with the world's problems.

[1] *Churches on the Move* by Gunnel Valquist, translated by Ingalill Hellman Hjelm (Fortress Press, Philadelphia 1970); p. 52

Poised between the world of childhood and the responsibilities of working life and yet dealing more wholeheartedly with general questions than they are ever likely to have a chance of doing again, they find it both an educational and a moral challenge and a release to take control of their own lives with others in this way. Inevitably such student communes rarely continue when their members graduate or leave college. And it would be dangerous if they did. It would be impossible to make any kind of guess as to how many such student communes there are and how many of them would claim to be christian. Student life today avoids such adjectives and the segregation implied in their use. But certainly christian students are in them and are learning much from them for the future.

There are, of course, more adult groups that follow the same pattern. An American writer describes 'one group of several couples that has just bought two big six-flat apartments in New Jersey, hoping to convert them into a commune. They think that the three or four members who now enjoy their work and make good money will be bringing in the "bread" for the group, while the rest of the adults will be painting, writing a novel, playing with children, and developing their personalities. They hope to live well with one big dining and recreation apartment, two refrigerators, two cars, and two vacation houses—a considerable reduction from their present level of consumer goods.'[1] This group may not be a specifically Christian one. But it is relevant as indicating that this interest in communal living is not restricted to students or the rebellious. The common characteristic of all these groups is that they live together in a house

[1] *What's Ahead For 1990* by John Platt, Associate Director of the Mental Health Research Institute at the University of Michigan; quoted from Vesper Exchange, September, 1972

The third group is less easy to define. It is composed of communities of people of all sorts, engaged in their own occupations, who meet regularly, share a common discipline and, to some degree, a common life. In some cases they maintain a central house for meeting and other activities and some of the members are engaged full-time in the administration. The rest live with their families in their own houses round about and are occupied in their own affairs. Commitment and the intensity of their discipline varies from group to group. They do not have the closeness of a commune sharing the one house. Nor do they have the parish affiliation typical of our first category. In some cases members retain their membership of their own local church. And, always, they tend to be ecumenical. Some groups are open to visitors who are welcome to share in the life of the group. Outsiders are often attacted by the sincerity of the discussion and by the strong sense of being a community. As the groups tend to be composed of families the age-range is wide, as are also the theological opinions and the ecclesiastical affiliations represented.

These three groupings, at least, indicate the variety of enterprises that may, willingly or unwillingly, be included under the name 'commune'. Examples could be given of groups very different in their way of organising their life and different in the purposes they are trying to serve, in the beliefs that bind their members together and in their attitude to the Christian faith. But they all represent attempts to find a freer, more satisfying and more corporate way of living for themselves. They are not primarily trying to prove anything. They are not directly trying to influence other people. They choose a way of life for themselves because this is what they want to do and feel that they ought to do and they will continue to do it so long as they find it suits them.

The moving cause for those who form these communes

has been dissatisfaction with the kind of life they already know and would otherwise have to live. They want to take some positive action to break away from life as they know it in nation, society and church. But perhaps their main dissatisfaction has been with family life as they have experienced it. The family in the West may not in recent centuries have changed so much in size as we have been tempted to think. But its economic position has radically changed. It is no longer a productive economic unit. Those who have jobs go out to work. The home has become the place of residence where a certain amount of leisure is spent. When the home is the centre of adult work it is a place of excitement and education for the children. When its main function becomes the care of small children it can become a cell in which many women and most children feel imprisoned. As young men and women become more and more involved outside the family in a rapidly changing world, they become painfully aware of the inadequacy of the family as they have known it as a preparation for life. Their dissatisfaction spreads into the rest of life. For the private isolation of the family dominates the other orders of society and above all the Church.

So some feel that they must break out and build a life of their own. Their dissatisfaction with the old and their strong conviction that it could have been much better are seen in their intention of creating a new pattern of domestic life. In a sense they are demonstrating what a modern family should be like. It must not be a prison cell, limited to the inmates. It must be the means of contact with other people. It must be a place where men and women learn to live together with those of all ages and different backgrounds and traditions. But it must be the common life of a family, dealing with time and money, meals and a house. It must not be a pretty life dealing only with what is nice and leisurely and respectable. It must be a physical and secular, political and economic unit. Its life must be open; open to discussion, free for the expression of all opinions, not dominated by a dogma. It must not be seen as an institution with rules or as an organisation with a cause. It is doubtful whether any group of people living together can attain to this purity of freedom. Some kind of discipline and methods of inter-dependence and of joint responsibility have to be built up. But this would be the ideal.

These experiments are of great significance for society and for the Church. They express a dissatisfaction and a desire which cannot be disregarded. Cynical criticism is easy. It is probably true that many communes are started because it is cheaper for a group of families or of individuals to live together in a large house and that they are able to do things together that they could never do by themselves. But no experiment of any kind is likely to succeed unless it is economically feasible and economically attractive. An experiment into which people have put their own time and their own money is more likely to hold together than one financed by people outside. It can also be argued that these experiments are made by the more sophisticated members of society, such as students and graduates: in other words by men and women who are just as much the products of middle class society as are the evils against which they rebelled. But, on the whole, it has generally been those set free in some measure by education and with some economic stability who have made experiments and discoveries. And, if these experiments are to say anything to the Church, they will have to speak in middle-class terms to be heard and understood.

But have these experiments anything of value to say to the Church about the probable pattern of its life in the future?

They surely do.

The dissatisfaction with the kind of life offered to young

people by family, society and the Church which they express is too urgent to be overlooked. It is easy to dismiss the communes as adolescent, naïve and transient. They may, indeed, all have disappeared within a year or two. But if so the dissatisfaction will remain and become apathetic and therefore more dangerous. The Church seems sometimes to accept this dissatisfaction as the occupational disease of young people and even of its older members and to do nothing about it. It seems not to want to encourage its members to make experiments in social living. Above all it does not seem to realise that the dissatisfaction is not mainly with ecclesiastical life but with the life of society, and that their experiments are more concerned with how to live in the world than how to run the Church. For the Church to take them seriously would mean the end of the tidily organised uniform congregation. The congregation would give way to a number of diverse and ever changing groups, which would emerge and fade away and be a nightmare to any ecclesiastical administrator. For these groups would be concerned with the ordinary secular lives of their members. They would have less to do with doctrine than with action.

The communes sound a note of warning to the Church. But it would be fatal if the Church took them as the all-sufficient warning. The commune can be as much an escape as the congregation. In protesting their disgust at the life of society they may be withdrawing from proper changes in society into an isolated citadel of their own.

The Church is not an organisation. It is not a building. It is not a group of people trying to live their own life. Work to do and people to serve are more essential to the Church than organisation or building or a cosy life.

The commune is an exciting experiment but not a sufficient clue to the future life of the Church.

5   *Experimental groups in work and service*

IN THE OLD days when there were still foreign missionaries in China they were always interested to learn the impressions that visiting Chinese formed of Britain and particularly of the Church there. One, more candid than the rest, said that what surprised him was that the Church in Britain did nothing; it only talked. When they asked to see what the Church was doing they were invariably taken to a meeting to hear someone talk. They were bewildered even more than they were shocked.

Their bewilderment is now shared by many in this country. It has led some to drift away from the Church. It has led them to make experiments on their own. These experiments are different from those considered in the last chapter. The commune is the expression of the need felt by many to find for themselves and with others who share their views a simpler and more satisfying way of life than that offered by contemporary society. In the 1960's some talked of the need to learn 'to be the Church'. The commune echoed this intention, though in a simpler form—to be themselves, or just to be. And there are probably truths to be learned only in this self-conscious way. The experiments we are now to think of concentrate on action rather than on being. And action always brings us into contact with other people.

Our Chinese visitors, in criticising the Church in Britain for doing nothing but talk, were contrasting it with the Church they knew in China. There the Church ran hospitals, schools and colleges, taught the illiterate peasant to read, cared for the blind and undertook as much other social work as could be managed. These kinds of activities were at one time carried out by the Church in this country. It is no longer the Church's task to do them nor would we want to see the Church again doing them. But this does not mean that all that the Church now does is to talk, even though its spokesmen seem often happy to elevate the proclamation of words as its highest and indeed sole function. And it doesn't make much difference to call words 'The Word'.

But the Church deceives itself and frustrates its members and others by its concentration on talk. For in actual fact it is far more involved in action: and in two ways which it continually forgets. Its members work. There are indeed a large number of retired people in the Church, as in the country as a whole. And the Church, through all its denominations, runs one of the biggest business enterprises in the country, in terms of property, investments, offices and staff. Men know that they themselves are working. They know that the Church is an immense organisation which must be doing something. But many are bewildered and frustrated. They may not see a purpose in their own work. They are often dissatisfied with how it has to be done. They find it difficult to see how their Christian faith or indeed any other beliefs can be worked out in it. And the organisation of the Church; is it there just to keep the record-player going?

So some men and women are making experiments in their own jobs: how they can be made more satisfying and how they ought to work with other people. Others are trying out new ways of caring for and working with and, most important of all, living with other people. These experiments are few in number compared with the flourishing and fading crop of communes. And they attract little publicity. But it may well be that they will outlast them, just because they are dealing with work and other people. And so they may be more significant pointers to possible patterns for Christian living in the future.

First, the experiments concerned with daily work.

When the Chinese critic compared the Church in Britain and in China he was probably remembering how much his education in the Christian faith had come through working with other people in school and college and in all the many secular affairs of a struggling young community. And this is an experience that the fortunate few among us at home have shared through working in some co-operative institution—school or hospital or altruistic institution. It is an experience that the communities we have considered earlier and others like them have found quite essential. A daily routine of practical work was necessary for their foundation and continuance. Iona could not have done without the manual work of building. Taizé found its place through agriculture among other activities. St Julian's is unique in the help it gives its visitors and this is based on the daily work of house and garden that binds the little community together. Lee Abbey was started as a centre for evangelism. Its warden claims that its emphasis has now changed. It is now a community of eighty people who work in maintaining their estate and helping others through conferences and other activities. This is something that the Church has always known, through its religious orders and missionary agencies.

This experience has been given only to the favoured few. The great mass of the lay members of the Church have no knowledge of it. Men *have* found joy in their craft and satisfaction in their work. But the organisation of their work has become much more complex and far out of their control. The questions it raises cannot be answered by the individual morality of an earlier age. And the talk of the

Church seems to have little relevance outside the church building and the home. It is despair about the possibility of finding meaning in modern commercial life that has led some to look for a simpler life in a commune. But it is not a way open to the ordinary worker.

Many in the Church in the West in the middle decades of this century woke up to the fact that the Church in the previous century had failed to take adequate account of what was happening in industry and commerce and that its task now was to try to relate its faith to the life that most people, including the Church's own members, lived in industry and commerce. So arose what was known then as Industrial Mission. The name has now been dropped. The word 'mission' gave the impression that the Church was going to enter a foreign land, whereas the land was where its members lived and worked. It also gave the impression that the Church had something to say and knew how to say it, whereas it was soon apparent that the Church had all to learn about how the world worked and how its members lived. This desire to learn and to serve was evident in most countries of Europe and in North America. In Germany there was the work of Horst Symanowski at Maintz Kastel and in some of the Evangelical Academies, as, for instance, at Freidewald and in the Netherlands at Lay Centres such as Bentweld. In Britain there was the work pioneered by E. R. Wickham and now spread over England and Scotland; and in the United States, especially at Detroit and Boston. The aim of this work might be said to give to men in industry opportunity and confidence to discuss their own problems and to give the Church the chance to discover how it should function in the non-domestic, extra-parochial areas of urban life where most people spend a large portion of their lives.

This work has not led to the setting up of an alternative church or an alternative to the congregation. It is reluctant to prejudice the openness and universality of its approach. It does not wish to bring new divisions into industry, especially along religious lines. It has thus been hesitatnt even to form groups. These may develop. But, if they do, it will be at the desire of men in industry. It therefore cannot be said that we see any new pattern of Church life emerging. What we do see more clearly is the kind of life in which new forms of christian living have to be found.

This work takes its place with the other and larger organisations—Trades Unions, professional bodies and the like—whose aim is to help people to understand the peculiar problems of their tasks. It also has its place in the schemes of training people for their jobs. And such training does not affect only their working lives. It affects their total life, including their church life. Their church life has somehow to find a way of integration into this ordinary secular life.

It is obviously not enough just to fit in to patterns created by other people. If it is right that Christians make experiments in communal living, it is as essential that they should also make experiments in industrial life. Such experiments are still very few but they are being made. They arise out of the natural desire to see how the teaching of Jesus can be applied to industrial as well as to private life. Their aim is not to follow the line of the Bruderhof—to be detached from commercial life and self-sufficient. It is to take their place in the ordinary secular world with the hope of finding a different way forward in it. Inevitably the method is that of co-operation among all in the factory instead of competition and this is expressed in common ownership and common control. There are in Britain six industries working on this christian basis. All, except one, are small, and intentionally so as success depends on mutual personal knowledge and trust. The oldest one is the largest—Scott Bader—with a membership of some four hundred and a turnover of nearly £5 million. They are linked together in an organisation—Industrial Common-ownership Movement—and believe that they have an evangelical purpose. One of it leaders writes of the smaller factory in which he works: 'I would not claim any great breakthrough, only a piece of pioneering which may just disappear, or more hopefully may eventually be regarded a useful pointer.'

A pointer to the Church of the future? Hardly; but a pointer to what some members of the Church will have to be doing. It is hard to see British industry as a collection of small Christian co-operatives. But men and women must find the way to experiment in industrial life if the Church is to live in an urban industrial society. This is why these experiments, though infinitesimal, are important. The experiments for which the Church waits are those that lay people make in their own secular jobs. The Church has assumed that their job is not what nice people talk about. This will have to be changed if the Church is to find a relevant way of living in the future. The trouble is that this field of commerce and industry is right outside the concern of the average congregation and of the bureaucracy of the denomination. Is it too much to hope that the Church in its own administration should be experimenting in new ways of doing business? It has a big enough organisation and is diverse enough in its work to enable it to make significant experiments. It is hampered by a timorous responsibiity for the use of what it regards as other people's money. But surely it is the Church's money given to do its work. But because of this timidity the first experiments have to be made by those who are prepared to risk their own time and their own money.

These groups of people willing to make experiments in their own jobs are certainly the smallest in number. They probably present the biggest difficulties but may well in the

end be the most significant. Groups concerned with the ser-
vices of others have a better Press. They may help us better
to see the way ahead. But in their way of working they are
as strange in the eyes of the conventional Church as those
we have been considering. And the strangeness lies in their
acceptance of other people.

We now come to the experiments concerned with service. The history of the Church is illuminated by the stories
of those who have given themselves to the service of their
fellows and have identified themselves with their condition.
The most famous example is Saint Francis. He abandoned
all that life had given to him and became the brother of the
poor in their poverty and of the sick in their weakness. The
best known example of more recent times is Charles de
Foucauld, born in 1858 into an aristocratic French family,
an orphan at five, an officer in the army who gave up a
military career and went off to live a solitary life with a
muslim tribe in the deserts of North Africa. He had no
companions and he made no converts. All that he left
behind him was the dictionary on which he was working, a
legend and the unlikely prospect of a company who would
live the life he lived in simple sharing with the poor. Now
the Little Brothers of Jesus and the Little Sisters of Jesus
are scattered all over the world, living lonely lives in the
acceptance of other people and bound together in a common devotion.

It may seem difficult to move from these heroic
examples to the kind of experiments we need now to discuss. Perhaps the difficulty lies in our willingness to see
those whom Francis and de Foucauld served as the pitiful
and innocent victims of man's cruelty and indifference and
our unwillingness today to regard the drug-addict, the
drop-out, the young delinquent of the slums and even the
inhabitants of new housing areas in the same light. Or
perhaps the difficulty lies in the difference of the identifica-

tion demanded. Giving up position, wealth, power and comfort seems admirable in others. To give up our opinions is more than most of us will accept.

When we think of these groups and especially when we try to see their importance for the future life of the Church, we can usefully treat them under three headings: problems, youth and community development.

Those who have felt called to help people whom society regards as hopeless—the misfits, the drop-outs, the drug addicts—have found that they can help them only by accepting them and by offering them a place where they can feel at home. This means that those who are trying to help them also make this place their home and are prepared to be accepted in their turn. Such work has to be based on deeply held convictions, either theologically explicit or quite unexpressed. Many of the groups are evangelical in purpose. Others such as the Simon Community and its successors —the Cyrenians and St Mungo's—follow a different line. As Kenneth Leech writes: 'To the drug addict the Simon Community offered no preaching and no evangelism: simply acceptance, care and support. It was based on the theology of incarnation and identification.'[1]

The second heading deals with work that is less spectacular but uses the same methods of acceptance and non-direction. It is what now goes under the head of Youth and Community Service. It is not dealing with those who are in need of food, shelter or care at an elemental or abnormal level, but with those who are in need of opportunity, activity and responsibility—in other words with the average under-privileged youth of our cities. Its aim is to help young people to be themselves, with all the dangers that this involves. This is work that the Church on the whole

[1] 'Christianity in underground drug culture' by Kenneth Leech; *The Times,* September 9, 1972

admires and supports, but at a distance, as necessary social work but not as an expression of its own life.

These groups, both those dealing with problems and those dealing with ordinary young people, work on the principle of acceptance: that no one can hope to help any one unless he is able to accept him as he is. This is the one help they need in order to be able to help themselves. This non-directive approach is not easy for those brought up in the Church or indeed in our society. The Church knows that it is commissioned to proclaim the truth. Our education has been based on instruction. Industry is controlled by directors. For a group to act on the principle of letting people be seems to many a waste of time and, worse, an encouragement to them to remain as they are.

Those who make these experiments have to find their vision and their endurance in strongly held views both as to principle and as to method—the acceptance of people as they are and a non-directive approach. They find their strength in the fellowship of those with whom they work and with those for whom they work. It is here that they find what others hope to find in the Church. And often they find it a strange business to go back to visit an ordinary congregation. Something is missing.

The organisation of the groups we have been discussing is new and so is the language they use. But their inspiration, in the case of many of these organisations, is not new. The life and teaching of Jesus have acquired for them a new and illuminating relevance. This is exemplified for them in the example of such men as Francis and de Foucault. It has found support in much modern psychological and educational theory. The work of T. R. Batten is important here.[1] The post-war communities already mentioned and many others not mentioned helped

[1] See, for example, *The Non-Directive Approach in Group and Community Work* (Oxford University Press; 1967)

men to see the need of this kind of approach. These communities could not avoid receiving all sorts of people with personal problems. They found that their own shared life had something to offer those whose difficulties the ordinary congregation could not meet. Usually they saw this caring work as an unavoidable part of their work. As an example of this we could take the work for Borstal boys long carried out by the Iona Community and by the Othona Community. It is based on the same principles.

All these groups can be seen as therapeutic groups to help people in need of various kinds. Can we begin to see the whole Church as this kind of group and all people in this kind of need?

But these groups were outside the regular work of the local church. Their work was often supported by the local churches but did not directly affect their life. They were more likely to be a cause of trouble and controversy than of example. We move now to the consideration of attempts made to bring the life of the local church into contact with the rest of the population of its area. We want in particular to think of the life of the church in areas of development or of re-development. This, of course, includes most urban areas and therefore cannot be regarded as the Church working in special areas. This is to move into a much wider field than the rather retricted one of the particular groups we have been considering.

The field is wider because now it includes everybody. But when we consider the particular experiments that are being made in this wider field we soon realise that they follow the same principles and the same methods. When the Church moves into an area of new development or when it finds that its old parish is unrecognisibly changed through re-development, it is confronted by a choice. It can follow the time-honoured strategy of the Church of working *for* people, or it can begin a new life of living and working *with* people. If it follows the former course it will soon erect the old bastions of privilege, power and defensiveness that it has for long known. It will maintain a division between itself and other people. Indeeed as it gets to know its new neighbours better it may well draw the lines of division more clearly. Criticism and protest will be the breath of its life. It will be glad to do some things for some people. Sometimes it will be as glad to do some things against others. If it follows the second course it has much to learn. It has to learn to live and work with others in equality. And this is not an easy lesson for christians now to learn.

The experiments we must now consider work on the principle of the acceptance of all people of the area and of their right to be there. They also use the non-directive method of approach. They do not claim a right to tell other people what to do. They act on the assumption that they all together, church and others alike, must work out what kind of life they want to live and what kind of a place they want to live in. As George Lovell writes: 'The Church is seen, not as a perfect society of perfect people at work to put right an imperfect sinful world, but as a growing, developing, maturing, spiritual organism working within the growing, changing, developing, maturing wider community. Both world and Church are seen to be in need of renewal.'[1]

Three examples may be give, others could be given. In many places local churches or groups in the churches are working on the same lines. The three we mention have the advantage of documentation.

The first is 'The Church and Community Project 70–75'. This, to quote its literature, is 'an ecumenical project designed to explore the practical, technical and

[1] *The Church and Community Development: an Introduction* by George Lovell (Grail and Chester House Publications 1972); p. 33

theoretical implications of the Churches becoming involved in community development.' The project is staffed by a team of Anglicans, Roman Catholics and Methodists, who are laying plans for a practical experiment in a chosen area. They state their aim further: 'We believe that an integral part of the mission of the Christian Church is to build community, promoting loving relationships between God and man, and man and man. We think that one very important way in which the Church can discharge its responsibilities in these areas is by becoming involved in community development. . . . It is through involvement in this process of meeting needs and improving their surroundings that people can develop and mature as individuals and establish new and deeper social relationships with each other. It is also through this process, so far as the Church involves itself in it, that church and neighbourhood can grow together.'

The Project 70–75 owed much to practical experience gained in our second example—the Parchmore Methodist Church Youth and Community Centre, at Thornton Heath in Surrey. This is not the beginning of new work in a new development area. It represents rather a change of direction for an established Methodist church to meet the needs of its own changing area. Their experience is very fully documented for us by reports which were not prepared for outside propaganda but for the on-going education of their members. They testify to the careful and lengthy preparations that have to be made to effect the change of direction. There has first of all to be the decision to make the change. Then there has to be meticulous education of the members of the church in their understanding of what is involved in the scheme and in their co-operation in working it out. This is achieved through week-end residential conferences and through the distribution for study of full reports. What is being achieved is not only an understanding of the surrounding community but also the formation of a community in the church. It is by facing the questions of their own lives that they begin to appreciate that the questions that other people face in their lives are the same.

The third example is of the transformation of a Victorian Presbyterian Church in North London (now known as the Manor Road United Reformed Church) into something new and strange. The building and land, all but a small part on which to build a small church unit, were sold to an independent but closely related housing society, who built twenty-eight housing units 'which accommodate a range of people including young families in three- and two-bedroom units and elderly people in bed-sitters, as well as two married couples in one bedroom units. There are West Indians, a Jewish couple, a Turkish Cypriot family, an Italian family, a Nigerian Youth and Community Worker with a Norwegian wife, and the usual mixture of English, Scottish and Irish people. They vary considerably in what work they do and what income they have.' And the Church is there in the middle, with no authority but open and available.

These experiments see their involvement in the local community development not as a new and extra bit of evangelistic work but as their life.

The experiments we have mentioned in this chapter, few and insignificant though they may appear to some to be, present the Church with a challenge. The challenge lies not so much in the question of why the Church is not doing what they are doing, as in a call to new thinking. These experiments seem off-centre because the Church in its theology, as least since New Testament times, has never seriously considered the questions these experiments are trying to answer. What is the place of all men in the Christian scheme of things or, to put it better, in God's world?

What should the Christian's attitude be to other men, especially to those of different beliefs and opinions? Do we believe in the Spirit at work in all men? And how does the Church regard men's daily work and the work of the world? If we go back with an open mind to the teaching of Jesus then answers do not seem hard to find. But classical theology has been confined by the concept of Christendom—the limited portion of the world that acknowledged the authority of the Church. It has therefore been almost exclusively concerned with a domestic discipline suitable for those inside and able to be enforced by an accepted authority. In this and the last centuries, when the idea of Christendom has been seen to crumble, Christian thinking has been dominated by the idea of the local congregation with its interests limited to the private and domestic life of the members. The place of work in the lives of men and women and the place of all in the mission of the Church are new topics, at least in their dimension and setting. The truth about them won't be found simply by going back to the great thinkers of the past—but in action. And this involves new thinking. As Robert Lecky and Elliott Wright tell us; we have to move 'towards a refusal to allow the institutional Churches total right to determine what the christian gospel is or how its mission should be shaped.'[1]

[1] *Can These Bones Live? The Failure of Church Renewal* by Robert E. Lecky and H. Elliott Wright (Sheed and Ward, New York 1969); p. 184

6   *Alternative churches*

MOST OF THE experiments that we have been considering have not taken to themselves the name of 'Church'. Some, indeed, are carried out by men and women who are members of the Church and who do what they are doing because of their faith. But they would see what they are doing simply as the work of a group doing something together. They would hope that what they were doing would be appreciated by the Church and have its interest and support. They might even hope that the Church might learn something from them and follow their lead on a larger scale. But they would be too modest to claim that they were acting in the name of the Church. Others would be more detached. They would prefer to be seen as quite on their own. Others again would be so critical of the Church that they would not want people to think that they had anything to do with it. They would feel that the word 'Church' had too many unhappy associations with the past and evoked too many prejudices to be other than an obstacle to their work. They would be glad to be free of it. So to most of those engaged in these experiments it would never occur, either from modesty or from pride, to take to themselves the name of 'Church'. They would see their actions as too personal, too particular and too temporary.

But there are other enterprises, of which some are quite as experimental, who gladly use the name. They claim to be the Church. Some would even claim not merely to be part of the Church but to be the only true Church, the only Church worth considering. All would see themselves as alternative Churches, as the only possible Churches in place of the defeated, respectable and lifeless institutions which they see around them. They are certainly alternatives. But as certainly they are Churches. They go their own way. But it is a way marked with the familiar milestones of worship, organisation, theology and, as often as not, internal division.

It is perhaps significant that the most conspicuous of these alternative Churches are American. It is true that it is easier to start an alternative Church now in America than it is in Europe. America still maintains a tradition of new beginnings. There is a constant urge to start afresh. It is no shame to have no roots. Men are accustomed to change their ecclesiastical allegiance. There is not the traditional, time-honoured image of the Church, reinforced, as in Europe, by a constitutional link with the State. On the other hand 'in the United States the Churches have, from the beginning, been much more wedded to the status quo, to the "manifest destiny" of the nation than in Britain.'[1] Men have been aware of the place of the Church and of its identification with the State. This has meant that dissatisfaction with the state of society has been directed against the Church. It has also meant that rebellion can take the form of creating another Church. Strange as it may appear America cannot get away from the fact of the Church as easily as men can in Europe. So new and alternative Churches are accepted as part of the accustomed scene. They arise quickly and perhaps they become conventional just as quickly.

But more lies behind the recent creation of new alternatives to the historic Churches. Their rise is without doubt due to the tragic problems in America and the turmoil they have brought: racial conflict and the demand for civil rights for all, the disparity between rich and poor not only

[1] *The Underground Church* edited by Malcolm Boyd (Sheed and Ward 1969); p. vii

in the rest of the world but in America, and above all the
long tragedy of Vietnam with its appalling suffering and
loss of life. In the founding of alternative Churches men
and women were expressing their shocked rebellion at the
failure of the historic Churches to deal in any adequate
way with these problems or even to be so concerned as to
alter their way of life. Behind the desire to find an alternative Church lay frustration at the respectability, self-
satisfaction and insensitivity of the Church as they knew it
and the conviction that the Christian Church was meant to
be something different. Renewal would be too slow a
business; and, indeed, if it could be achieved it might be
only a refurbishing of the old, getting it to act a little more
efficiently and for a little longer.

So in America we find many examples of alternative
Churches. Though their setting is so different, they have
still something to say to us in Britain. They all reflect in
varying degrees the same despair of the old and the same
desperate hope. We can mention only three examples.
They are chosen because they are different in themselves,
different in their style of life, different in their attitude to the
older Churches, and different in the extent to which they
are a response to the political situation. But, however op-
posed to each other, they are at one in claiming the name
of Church.

Our first example may seem, at first sight, to have little
to do with political protest. The Pentecostal Churches are
associated with fundamentalism, individualism and detachment from secular life. But, as the historian of
Pentecostalism writes: 'The origins of the Pentecostal
movement go back to a revival amongst the negroes of
North America at the beginning of the present century.'[1]
So the movement is recent though, of course, its special
manifestations go back a long way. Pentecostalism,

[1] *The Pentecostals* by Walter J. Hollenweger (SCM Press, 1972); p. xvii

therefore, arose out of the sufferings of slavery and the subsequent awakening of the sufferers to their right to a life of their own. Their suffering and their eschatological hopes found outlet in the negro spirituals. Their religious independence was expressed in the Pentecostal movement. They had to be free of the hierarchical organisation and intellectual sophistication of the ruling white Churches. They needed a religion that was both individual and sociable in which they were able to express joy, sorrow and hope without restraint. It was a religion for the depressed and the dispossessed. It spread quickly and widely in South America and in Africa.

These Pentecostal churches, independent and fundamentalist, with many divisions and only loosely related to each other, were not alternatives but the only churches their members had known. When today we think of Pentecostalism as an alternative Church in Britain, we are thinking of something a little different. It is sometimes called neo-Pentecostalism. It is seen in a rapid growth of an interest in the Spirit in the historic Churches of Britain and America. It expresses itself in much the same way as in the older Pentecostalists. Speaking with tongues is seen as the primary and generally essential gift of the Spirit. No adequate explanation is given why of all the gifts of Penteost escstatic utterance is put above the ability to speak to people in language they can understand or willingness to have all things in common. It may be that it is so treasured as the individual's assertion of personal praise and thanks.

But there are differences. It does not spring from black suffering. It rests on white comfort. It is looking for freedom, but a different freedom. It seeks freedom from the formality and caution of the established Churches. It challenges paternalistic authority. It claims the right of an individual to speak for himself or herself. It is conservative in theology but unconventional in behaviour. It welcomes the use of music and art, sometimes in odd forms. It offers a joy and even a violence in worship that offends the staid but stimulates the young. Many of its members are interested in science, biblical scholarship and politics. But on the whole the discussion of the world's problems takes up little of their time. For all these reasons Pentecostalism may prove to have a firm foothold in the life of the Church in the immediate future. And this may well be because the Pentecostals of this type do not seek to set up an alternative Church but rather to change the existing Church from the inside.

Our second example is very different. It does not belong to a different tradition from the main Churches. It has, indeed, come into being as a separate, new Church. Those who have founded the new Church have done so not so much out of violent criticism of other Churches as out of a sense of their own failure to live the Christian life and of the need to do something positive about it. The Church of the Saviour in Washington, DC, is an entirely new and independent Church. It recognises its place in the ecumenical movement. It is connected with the National Council of Churches of North America and with the World Council of Churches. It maintains friendly relations with its neighbouring congregations. But it goes its own way as an entirely independent Church, responsible to no bishop, ecclesiastical authority or denomination. It is founded on a very demanding discipline of membership: a two year educational probation, and a commitment to economic giving, to work and to worship which must be renewed every year. One who visited it in the early days and stayed in its house and shared in retreats at its estate of Dayspring can never forget the quiet intensity of its fellowship or his amazement at the work that its membership of some seventy members undertook in running a coffee house, an art centre and a renewal centre for people in extreme need—in addition to the full programme of activities for members and others at their house in the city and at their estate in the country. The one thing they did not do was to build and maintain an ecclesiastical building exclusively for worship. Their large house on Massachusetts Avenue is advertised as the headquarters of the Church not as the Church. The Church is the small group of deeply committed people.

The Church has grown since then. After eight years it had two hundred and fifty members[1] and is presumably still growing. It has developed its work, action and service. It is always ready to embark on new enterprise which it calls a 'mission' and its members are expected to serve in one of these. Particularly striking has been their work for deprived children in Washington. But even more than to action they are committed to the cultivation of the spiritual life of their members. And sometimes the two seem to be in conflict.

The Church of the Saviour is a living example of what any congregation in any Western city might do. It has advantages. It enjoys freedom from outside control. It enjoys the independence of making its own decisions unhampered by the fear of involving others. And above all it enjoys wonderful and unique leadership. But perhaps it pays a price. It is not burdened with the corporate sense of guilt which belonging to a larger body brings. And so perhaps it lacks some of that identification with those in need which is the mark of some of the older experiments. Perhaps its discipline is not in strident enough colours to appeal to dissatisfied youth. It has certainly shown the kind of discipline the Church could demand of its members and has given a new direction to its service. But it has not perhaps questioned enough the conventional expressions of the

---

[1] *Journey Inward, Journey Outward* by Elizabeth O'Connor (Harper and Row 1968); p. 53

beliefs of the Church. It has not ventured into any new meaning of the Christian faith for the world today. Perhaps it would not be too much to say that it is an alternative Church for those already deeply committed to the Church. It is possible that congregations on fire with some new vision will follow its example by becoming independent Churches. But there is little evidence so far of its example being followed.

The third example that claims the name of Church is again quite different. Its name is clearer than the thing itself. It's a strange name and used with many different meanings—the Underground Church. And it's not a nickname given to it but its chosen name. It is presumably adopted in opposition to the Church above ground, established, endowed and property owning, visible, static. It carries undertones of rebellion, of plotting, of unseen activities. But it is quite anxious to be visible. It enjoys good publicity. It offends the staid and the state in taste, in opinion and in activity. But it is not violent. It represents the angry young men and women of the Church. But it is no angry brigade. And it is American.

As a contemporary phenomenon it is neither uniform nor organised. We can recognise it in at least three distinct forms.

First there are those who chose to go underground. They said a lot about what it meant to be underground. But they did not talk about 'the underground church'. They were of the Church and they knew that they had to go underground and that this was where the Church was. Their conspicuous representatives are Philip and Daniel Berrigan, brothers and Jesuits, and the latter a poet of note. In May 1968 they, with others, invaded a government office in Catonsville, Maryland, seized service records and burnt them. Sentenced to three years imprisonment, they managed to go underground. Some, including Philip, were soon caught and imprisoned. Daniel existed for months 'underground', meeting his friends, speaking at meetings, appearing on TV, interviewed by the Press. And then he was caught and imprisoned. Their life underground could be called 'the Church Underground', because they found the Church there with a new meaning and a new hope. Politics became more vividly of the faith. 'I am convinced,' wrote Daniel Berrigan from underground, 'that contemplation, including the common worship of the believing, is a political act of the highest value, implying the riskiest of consequences to those taking part. Union with the Father leads us, in a sense charged with legal jeopardy, to resistance against false, corrupting, coercive, imperialist policy. The saints were right: their best moments were on the run, in jail, at the edge of social acceptability.'[1] It recalls the catacombs. It is new for the Church in America. Their action at Catonsville was in protest against the war in Vietnam. But 'underground' meant identification with all those who had no say in their lives. 'Liberation, education, consciousness; if I'm learning anything it is that nearly everyone is in need of these gifts . . . I think of all those we so easily dismiss, whose rage against us is an index of the blank pages of their lives, those to whom no meaning or value has ever been attached by politicians or generals or churches or universities or indeed anyone, those whose sons fight the wars, those who are constantly mortgaged and indebted to the consumer system; and I think also of those closer to ourselves, students who are still enchanted by careerism and selfishness, unaware that the human future must be created out of suffering and loss.'[2]

This is no likely pattern for the Church. It is, we hope, a temporary experience. But it has an abiding word for the

[1] *America is Hard to Find* by Daniel Berrigan (SPCK 1973); p. 78
[2] ibid pp. 94, 95

Church, on a par in Europe with Dietrich Bonhoeffer's political action and execution.

This was the Church defying the State and finding its life only underground. This is for the few, though the challenge is to the many. The second form of the Underground Church is made up of those who feel compelled to get out of the above-ground building of the Church into the life of the people. As Malcolm Boyd writes: 'The Underground's main task is to look *outside* Church structure, to see the people in the world and love them.[2] It is composed of men and women who cannot find a satisfying and sufficiently demanding life for themselves in the ordinary life and service of the Church. Many of these are priests and nuns who have given up their ecclesiastical calling but have not given up their faith. Others have found with them a more vital worship and a deeper sense of purpose in meeting in secular buildings and with those of other opinions. If by a Church we mean a group meeting for worship in the name of Jesus and in his service of others, then this is a Church. Its marks are freedom in worship and co-operation with all without question. It is not so much an underground Church, for it is not trying to hide or to escape or to plot, as a Church on the ground, at the grass roots, unprotected, open to the wind of heaven and to all comers. Its leaders are mainly Roman Catholic. They are more certain of what they are protesting against and their actions are more conspicuous. They are, perhaps, also more insistent on the central place that worship, in some form, must hold. But this underground Church is essentially ecumenical. It welcomes those of all denominations and of none. It is a *free* Church which sees itself part of the one Church.

This free Church merges into the work of those who know that they can only reach others by being on the

[1] *The Underground Church* edited by Malcolm Boyd (Sheed and Ward 1969); p. 5

ground or undergrund. They know that they can only reach others by being outside the Church because they know that this is where they belong themselves. But sometimes the Church sees them as useful evangelists and is willing to support their work. As one critic has observed: 'Our image of the underground Church is misleading if it depicts a movement which exists independently of the established churches. The spontaneous movement is by and large composed of people who have been formed in the Churches and often retain active membership in them even in a ministerial capacity. The experimental groups draw recruits and monetary support from the Churches even for supposedly anti-establishment activities and exist physically, morally, and structurally in a love-hate relationship with their parent churches.'[1]

The word 'underground' implies escape from the conventional, protest against the established and rebellion against the status quo. Can it survive to build its own lasting structure? Or will it want to? Vietnam forced it into being. But Vietnam was only the glaring symbol of other wrongs. But can protest become a pattern? Or rather can the positive values for which it stands invade and take over the Church? Who can say? In any case it is primarily a question for the American Church.

For this underground can scarcely be said to exist in Britain. There are, of course, the protesters. There are the lapsed priests and nuns. There are the rebel Protestants who would like a Church outside the Church. But they seem less committed than the Americans to the idea of the Church, less anxious to start a new Church, less rebellious perhaps, ready to wait as Europe has learned to wait rather than to change.

The only visible sign of the underground is in a

[1] 'Spontaneous Groups in the United States' by James J. Arraj, in *Trends* for December, 1972, p. 57

magazine—*The Catonsville Roadrunner*. The title reveals its inspiration. But Catonsville is far from England and the road it wants to run is hardly that of dodging the police. It serves a useful purpose in expressing youth's revolt. It gives news of what is happening. It stimulates thought on certain issues. But apart from this, its aim seems to be to shock the Church by its language rather than to defy the State by its actions.

But it shares with the underground Church in all its forms the intention to find a more radical way of life. It challenges not only the respectability and complacency but also the political conservatism of the Church. It wants to see the Christian faith expressed not only in more positive action but also in more vehement joy.

These three types of alternative Churches—the Pentecostal, the independent Church of the Saviour and the Underground Church—are very different in themselves but they have certain things in common. They appeal to those who are dissatisfied with the Churches as they are. They adopt a severe discipline of action. They agree in not repudiating the Church but instead in claiming to be the Church. They are also united in a new interest in Jesus. They reveal this in very different approaches. The Pentecostals would almost seem to put Jesus secondary to the Spirit. But undoubtedly concentration on Pentecost, even if mainly on one aspect of it, does lead to interest in the New Testament and in Jesus. The Church of the Saviour goes back very definitely to the Jesus of the Gospels. Their discipline reflects the experience of Jesus and his twelve disciples. The activities to which they are committed are corporate rather than individual. The Underground Church would see Jesus outside the Church as the suffering servant, the rejected and crucified, the man for others.

But this interest in Jesus is not confined to these new

alternative Churches. It must seem odd to speak of an interest in Jesus as new and remarkable in the Church. But it has not always been a constantly conscious interest in the Church. It has been awakened at times of political and economic change and of dissatisfaction with the path that the Church seems content to follow. So it is not surprising that at the present time this interest should be manifest. What is surprising is the width of the interest, the forms in which it is expressed and, above all, that it is peculiarly among young people. It is so general that people can talk about a Jesus Movement. It can almost claim inclusion with the alternative Churches. Its origin was in America. It arose out of, and is fed by, the same sense of frustration, rebellion and dissatisfaction with the way of life of Church and society. And as these are not confined to the United States, the movement has spread to other countries. It does not have or attempt to have any organisation. But for many it is their Church.

There are different and contradictory groupings in the movement. There was the first group of rebels, drug-addicts and drop-outs who turned to Jesus as a new experience and found something. Then there were the groups of more serious seekers who were looking for a way of life and found it in the teaching of Jesus. They were prepared to give up family, possessions and work to live as they felt that Jesus lived with his disciples. They witnessed to their way of life and to what they had learned of Jesus. Then there were groups, conservative, disciplined, evangelistic, who saw this as their way of life and witness. There is no reason to doubt the sincerity of any of these groups. But other people have tried to help them or to use them or to exploit them.

But in all the groupings of the movement three things are common.

They are all outside the organisation of the Church and

resistant of its jurisdiction. They rarely think of using church buildings. Their place is on the ground, in the street, among people.

Then they do not conform to the conventional life of their elders, either in dress or in manners. They want to find simplicity in their way of living.

And thirdly they express their point of view and their sense of freedom not in intellectual forms to be argued but in song and music to be enjoyed. They may use fundamentalist language but their way of life is free.

What is their picture of Jesus? Who can say? The only question is whether it is true for them and whether it will last. But the word to the Church is unquestionable. We cannot now avoid taking Jesus seriously.

7   *The favourite alternative*

FOR MANY THE alternative to the Church as they have known it is not another kind of Church but no Church at all. They are not hopefully looking for some new type of Church. Nor are they prepared desperately to make a deliberate experiment of their own. They just stop going to church. Often they have been so casual about it that to their surprise they find that they have not been to church for a very long time and that they haven't missed it. They may sometimes have an uncomfortable feeling that perhaps they ought to go. But in the end they don't and they're perfecty happy. The Church has ceased to mean anything to them. They have found a pleasant alternative—just not to go. And not to go to church is taken to mean to have no part in the Church.

They are a vast company. And they are not all the same. Some try to find excuses because they feel a bit guilty. Most say nothing at all. Their silence is the most eloquent confession of where they stand. Others might be more vocal. They do not wish to pretend. They feel that to continue nominal membership is to indulge in a fraud. The words dear to the Church have come to mean little to them. All this talk about Anglicans and Methodists and Presbterians and the concern about organisation seem to them meaningless. They are weary of the Church.

None of these varied people have come to a great decision, religious or theological. They do not feel that anything has happened to them at all. Loyal churchmen might accuse them of drifting with the tide of popular opinion. But most of them would claim that they had not altered their opinions in the least. They had not come to the shattering decision that the Christian faith is meaningless nor even to the deliberate opinion that the Church is irrelevant. They certainly would not call themselves atheists. They take for granted that they are Christians. They would be insulted if any one suggested otherwise. They might be at a loss to explain what being a Christian means. But their attempt might not be very different from the explanation of many church-attenders. They might, if they were roused, add that they were at least as good Christians as some who go to church. They would probably describe the Christian faith as a way of life rather than as the acceptance of a particular doctrine. It's the matter of going to church that perplexes them. By their absence they ask the question: Why is it so important to go to church? They know at least that it's not enough.

There are, of course, a few who have left from a profound conversion to unbelief. And there are also undoubtedly a few who refuse any longer to go to church because of their conviction of what the Christian faith really means. They feel that the life of the Church is an affront to the faith it professes. But of these there are very few, and they are more likely to be found in the far-out experiments than among those who are content to do nothing.

But when we try to think of the people who have given up 'going to church', some things are fairly certain. One is that we cannot attempt to count them. There are too many of them and they are too indefinite. Any all-embracing description of them is impossible. Their multitudinous numbers run off into all shades. There are those who are still recognised as members of their local church which they never attend. Some do so with uneasy regret. They belong to the company that Graham Greene knows: 'many of us abandon Confession and Communion to join the Foreign Legion of the Church and fight for a city of which we are no longer full citizens.'[1] There are those, on the other hand, who would be shocked and irritated at being described as lapsed church-members. Another thing certainly is that, although they are by far the largest group of those seeking alternatives, they are completely unorganised. They do not form groups. They do not organise meetings. Some do, indeed, go to meetings and join groups but these are ordinary secular meetings and groups. So the sociologist cannot collect facts or statistics about them. The communes, however rebellious, are institutional and reportable compared with them.

But they are not any the less real on this account. Perhaps they remain more real just because they cannot be categorised. They are people, not figures on a chart. They are just people. This is what they want to be.

The one thing we cannot do with them is to dismiss them. We dare not say that they are not important because they are not organised or cannot be systematically described. Nor can they be regarded as irresponsible or thoughtless or lacking in seriousness. Their numbers make them typical. The positions they occupy make them important. The essentially negative quality of their attitude to the Church and the vagueness of their opinions and hopes should make them of supreme interest to all concerned with the future of our society and of peculiar interest to those anxious about the future of the Church.

These men and women would hesitate to use the designation 'christian' only because it is assumed to mean 'going to church'. And this is what they will not do. They have not failed the Church. The Church has failed them. For the Church knows no obligation of men to the Church. It knows no obligation save its own to love all men. Those

[1] *A Sort of Life* by Graham Greene (The Bodley Head 1971); p. 166

who have rejected the Church may be called of God to live outside the Church for their good and for the Church's good. Their calling may be to find, at great risk to themselves, how to live as Christians in our new open, secular world. If the Church were composed only of those who found in it all that their hearts desired it would be a truly terrifying institution, unable to reflect much of the love of Jesus and quite unable to lead its members out in mission and service.

In a recent book J. W. Stevenson rejoices that there are still plenty of these fringe people in the Church. 'The presence of the apparently casual and formal member, against much influence which might keep him away, may be a sort of judgement against our rectitude—a rectitude which does not look for anything new, anything more wonderful, anything more demanding, anything which would be a power to change us as well as other people. We may not appear to believe anything more than he does. He sees us holding on, without much thought, to the practices, the forms of thought, the language, the existing shape of the Church, with minds closed against any new thing God may be requiring of us.'[1] If these members inside the Church have something to say which the Church disregards at its peril, their much more numerous representatives outside have something even more serious to say.

They are a reminder to the Church of the society in which we all live. In a sense they are a reminder to the Church of what the true membership of the Church is. They are certainly a revelation—for it has long passed out of the Church's memory—that the life of the Church is not contained by ecclesiastical buildings; that even the worship of the Church is not expressed only through its formal acts of worship; that Christian life is lived outside.

[1] *God outside the Church* by J. W. Stevenson (Saint Andrew Press 1972); p. 10

They are, in other words, the constant reminder that the world is the object of God's love and purpose; that it was in the world that Jesus lived; that, indeed, he knew the world but never knew the Church. The Church is the herald, the earnest and one of the instruments of God's purpose for all men. And it is so only as it forgets itself.

These unwilling renegades have a sound theological case which they would rarely dream of expounding. They see their attitude as negative because this is how others describe it. They do not feel that they have a right to say anything on their own. But, although they would not want to talk theology, they have some valuable theological insights.

They know that what in the end matters is what goes on in the world, not what goes on in the church. They know that if God can be known as real it will be in the world that he will be so known. They feel that what the Church does should point to this and they don't see that it does, at least for them. Probably they feel that the affairs of their family, their neighbours, their work, their community, their world are more important to them, and probably to God. They would not use such words. But if they think of God at all they do so in personal and universal terms: as somehow the creator of all and somehow the father of all men. Because of this they feel that they are inside God's purpose, not outside. The exclusive attitude of the Church offends their religious sense. They know that it does not agree with their picture of Jesus. And they do have a picture of him. It may be naïve or sentimental, but it is there, a real picture for them. It is formative of their criticism of the Church and of their own idea of how men ought to behave.

It would be wrong to suggest that they are bereft of all help and without any means of grace. They are aware that in the Church they did not find adequate help. This is why

they left. They are perhaps not expecting to find it outside.
But they are not without their courses of instruction, their
agencies of spiritual direction and even their fellowship. We
should not overlook the help they get from TV, radio,
books and adult education classes. These offer intelligible
ways by which people are sustained in their interests and
learn what other people are doing and thinking in a way
unknown to previous centuries. And help and grace always
come mainly through our fellowmen.

We have no right to say that these people lack a
theology. We cannot say that any one who thinks about
life has no theology, unless by theology we mean academic
information about what people in the past have said. This
is a luxury they would never claim. Yet their theology, if
too uninstructed to deserve the name and, indeed, too simple to express all their questions, is yet based on assump-
tions that are fundamental to the Christian faith.

The Christian faith is based on three convictions which
can be stated very simply or very abstrusely. There is the
belief that this is God's world, that somehow it serves his
purpose and that therefore we can have hope. Then there is
the belief that the life, teaching and death of Jesus not only
indicate the nature of this hope but even now breaks down
divisions and allows men now to know unity. And thirdly
there is the conviction that men are enabled by their very
humanity to be involved in this hope. The faith of the great
unchurched is a very simple acceptance of belief in God, in
Jesus and in the human spirit. It is a trinitarian faith stated
in the simplest, crudest terms. It seems to have no need of
sacraments, or of any corporate expression of failure and
forgiveness, though without question most people are only
too well aware of failure in their own lives and, gratefully,
of the forgiveness of their fellows. In other words they
know no need of the Church. They would not go so far as
the talk of Chirstian faith without the Church. But they

would certainly assert that there can be Christian life without the Church.

It would be difficult for any one to prove that this simplistic faith is heretical. It would be easier to argue that to deny these three beliefs is heretical. To state that the world is in the power of evil, or that Jesus divides men into the good and the bad, the saved and the damned, or that there is no creative spirit at work in all men: this would be heresy. It is probable that this sense of the unity of creation, of the unity of mankind and of the unity of the spirit will come to be seen as the irreplaceable foundation of faith for men in the world of the future.

In a recent book Colin Morris could be said to be stating this faith passionately, if to some shockingly, when he wrote: 'I am more than a Methodist, more than a Protestant; yes, even more than a Christian. I am first and foremost a member of the human race, and to that must be my primary allegiance. So I have only one *ecclesia*—mankind. There is only one true baptism, which is birth, and only one true sacramental table—at which every member of the human race will some day sit by right *and be fed*. Every other so-called sacrament is a parody of these true sacraments, just as our institutional Churches are a parody of the true *ecclesia*.'[1] Colin Morris is a minister and a loyal servant of the Church. He is expressing his view of the essential Church. But what he says will be more congenial to many outside the Church than to some inside.

But the world of the future belongs more to the innumerable people outside than to the congregations that make up the Church as we know it today. They are at home in it. And they can help the Church to find its place with men in it. As the world becomes more inter-dependent

[1] *Mankind My Church* by Colin Morris (Hodder and Stoughton 1971); p. 73

and its people more intermingled in work and at play, men and women will become more and more detached from the stable little communities in which up to now they have felt at home. The close-knit village has ceased to exist. The local congregation becomes rather odd and pointless to people constantly on the move. The small, local, stable group will, of course, always be appreciated by some—by those permanently settled in one place and by the retired. Those whose education has sent them from home and whose work has kept them mobile will gravitate to the company of those who share this kind of life. The groups concerned with work or service and even the most ephemeral of groups may well be much more attractive than the congregation.

The silent absence, with a few occasional outbursts, of these many people from the Church is expressing things of vital importance to the Church of the future. It is revealing something of the life that we, those inside as well as those outside the Church, are living. It is saying; this is your world and you can't shut it out. It also shows how unsatisfying many find the present life of the Church. They want something more personal and more obviously related to the life they live and the people with whom they work. This desire may lead them into queer company—of the esoteric, the occult or the plain faddy. But the desire to find something personal and to escape from what is uniform is healthy, and a rebuke to the Church. And they are suspicious of dogmatic statements. Their escape from the Church is probably due most of all to resentment at being told what they must believe. They think they know. They certainly don't want to be told.

They don't need the Church. At least they don't need the Church they have known. But are they looking for another Church? The company of all men of goodwill? Will they build up some pattern of social living that will support them in this quest? It is possible. And what should be the Church's attitude to such an attempt? Probably not to try to entice them back. But to try to recover some aspects of the Christian faith that they are feeling after and that the Church seems to be overlooking: the unity of the world, the unity of all men and the unity of the Spirit.

At least if we are seriously to see what are the alternatives to the present pattern of the Church's life and to learn from them, then this is the one, above all others, that we must not overlook. For it is the favourite.

8 *The church that we know*

INEVITABLY WE COME back to the Church as it is, to the Church that we know. We cannot say anything, however wild or however hopeful, about possible patterns for the Church in the future without considering the Church as we see it now. It remains the biggest determining factor for its own future. The various enterprises that we have been discussing have arisen out of dissatisfaction with the Church as it is. Their originators have criticised the Church for what it is doing and for what it has failed to do. For instance they would say that the Church did nothing in protest against the great evils of the present time such as war, hunger, racial inequality but said much in protest against evils trivial in comparison such as pornography and gambling. But they knew that extravagant criticism was not enough. They knew that they had themselves to do something in despair or in hope: in despair of the Church doing anything new or hope that it would follow a lead. But all these experiments have been made in reaction to the Church. It is the Church that has determined the nature of the criticism. It is the Church that has involuntarily suggested the alternatives.

The Church is there in the background, just as the family is there in the background of most people's lives. However rebellious children are and however far they run, they never escape from the influence of their family. The Church is there in much the same way as the family, and in an even more positive way. Rebellious children escape in

the end by founding families of their own. It's more difficult
to found a Church of one's own. It is the one thing that
most of those who start experiments don't want to do. But
all the time they are looking over their shoulders at the
Church. They know that what they are doing must find a
lasting form if it is to succeed. And they cannot themselves
provide that universal form. Their criticism of the Church
is fierce just because it is there, ready-made, available, but
blind to its task and its opportunities, blocking the way into
the future. For behind the vehemence of their protest is the
conviction that some permanent and universal body of
men and women, free to love and to act and to suffer, is
needed. And if not the Church, then something very like
the Church. And if something like the Church, why not the
Church?

And the Church *is* there. Despite its losses and its
problems, despite rebellion and the seeking of other ways,
despite the attraction of all kinds of alternatives and the
greater attraction of doing nothing at all, the Church
remains, to all appearance unchanging, immovable, eter-
nal.

Some would say that it survives because of its
assets—its property, its man-power, its position of
privilege, its power. And no one will deny the help that
these offer to continuity, however much they may offend
some and satisfy others into repose.

But it is not on account of these that the Church survives. It might be more true to say that it survives in spite
of them. It survives because so many cannot do without it.
Brian Wicker, the Roman Catholic author, after stating
that there are many 'to whom the church, especially the
Roman Catholic Church, as actually experienced in its institutional form, is often an alien and even scandalous
irrelevancy' goes on to insist: 'But to experience the official
institutional church as an irrelevancy is by no means the

same thing as saying that it is expendable.'[1] Men may criticise it. They may abandon it. But they cannot exist without the idea of it, and the necessity of it. It's like the weather or one's family: so near that at times you cannot bear it, so essential that you cannot get on without it. The Church continues through all that happens because men want the security of something that stands for what they dare not themselves express; and because they cannot really believe in anything unless it is embodied in people. They know that the Church is not made up of buildings and officials, of money and of power, however indispensible and inescapable these things may appear to be. They know that the Church exists for what it is not yet. It exists because of a mystery—the mystery of life through Jesus and with other men. It must always be inexplicable why people hold on to the Church and how it survives. But this is true of all other things in life that matter and endure.

No one makes a discovery or tries an experiment who does not believe in a spirit of life that opens doors into new ways and leads into truth and life. The Church is to ordinary people the assurance that the spirit of God is at work in the world and that they are called somehow to cooperate with it. They may at times, and some very often, wonder whether anything is ever going to happen. But without the ideas that are so strangely expressed in its worship and, even more, without the contact it brings with others they would know no basis of reality for their faith. They would be tossing on a sea of uncertainty, and they would be very lonely.

But men cannot just wait for things to happen. Men cause changes and then have to react to them. For the Church this is part of its faith. To believe in God is to expect change. To know Jesus is to have an idea of the

[1] *First the Political Kingdom: A personal Appraisal of the Catholic Left in Britain* by Brian Wicker (Sheed and Ward 1967); p. xi

nature of change. The sin against the Spirit is the refusal to believe that things happen, new and fresh. The unpardonable sin for the Church is for it to believe that the pattern of its life is fixed; especially for the Church today to believe that the congregational pattern of life which is common to all denominations in the West is sacred and unchangeable. The one thing of which we can be quite certain is that the way by which Christians live changes from generation to generation. Death lies in being tied to the patterns of the past.

We must accept with gratitude that the Church is there and will continue. Its final extinction would be tragic to contemplate and impossible to conceive. Equally we must believe that it will change its form into something new and strange and its present institutional structure will change beyond recognition and even fade away.

The enterprises that we have been considering have something pertinent to say to the Church. The Church as presently organised has to be aware of them and to assess them and to learn from them. It is not only from them that the Church must learn. It has much to learn from enterprises quite outside the Church. But experiments that arise in protest against the Church have an insistent relevance.

The experiment of the commune aims at finding a personal, spontaneous, demanding and satisfying way of corporate living, based on the shared use of time and money. It is a judgement on the rather artificial, very selective life of the average congregation, which excludes from its concern anything to do with work, money or politics—the three topics which touch people most closely. It indicates how the Church must find a much more satisfying and demanding life for its members. The few experiments that have to do with men's Christian understanding of the purpose and method of their own jobs are an indication of the Church's lack of concern with what occupies much of the

energies of most men and causes most of their
anxieties—their work, and of its need to find the way of
being so cocerned in its local and organisational life. The
groups committed to the care of people in special need and
to the needs of ordinary people in difficult situations have
arisen out of the Church's lack of constant personal interest in other people than its own. The enterprises that
have not been afraid of the name 'church' remind the com-
placent Church how serious some people are in their hopes
for the Church. And lastly the multitudes who gladly do
without the Church and still call themselves Christians
recall the Church to the universality of the gospel and its
commitment to love.

Perhaps the most important thing that the Church needs
to recognise is that all these enterprises which arise out of a
christian concern, however odd and however critical, are
part of the total life of the Church. The Church cannot be
confined to those who are in possession. And the first duty
of those in possession is a welcoming hospitality.

For the Church the value of these experiments lies not so
much in the demonstration of new methods as in the in-
sight they bring to the Church into the world in which people live and an understanding of their hopes and fears. The
success of these experiments will not lie in their
perpetuating themselves as small, exclusive enterprises but
in the encouragement they give to the Church to change.
And this depends on the Church's willingness to learn, not
only from them but from the life of the world.

The Church is learning slowly, things are happening and
changes are taking place. These may not be very obvious.
They may seem very slow and quite unrelated to each
other. We must remember that we are dealing with
thousands of congregations, most of them small and all of
them conditioned not to take action. So that if a congregation does decide to do something, it can do only one thing

at a time and only a few of its members will really get involved. There can therefore never be a general strategy for the Church, however keenly the leaders of the Church may plan for one. Change in the life of the Church is like change in the life of the family; as certain in fact but as difficult to diagnose or prove. Generalisation becomes dangerous and selection unfair. We can however mention three types of activities which are to be found in many places. These illustrate changes in the life of the congregation and not merely new ways of carrying out old activities more efficiently, however admirable these may be.

Probably the best established change in the manner of life of a congregation has come about through the development of groups. This has been going on for quite a long time; so much so that it is now taken for granted. But it is a radical change. A generation or two ago the only groups to be found in a congregation—and indeed the only ones encouraged—were for the doing of a specific internal piece of work. Now in many congregations there are all kinds of groups which meet not necessarily to do work but probably for the interest or common concern of their members—for study, or discussion or just to be together. They challenge the old idea that nothing should be done in which every one is not free to join. They point to the fact that the congregation is made up of people with varied and even conflicting interests. They are a protest against the old idea of the member of the Church as one who attends and is attentive. Groups have led to members of a congregation coming to know each other more intimately and to know much more about the ordinary life of one other. The discussion of secular affairs and of the meaning of their faith has been made possible. It has thus been largely educational, preparing the congregation for a more active life. If this does not get an outlet it may leave people more frustrated.

Secondly there are the ecumenical projects that give hope for the breaking of the congregational and denominational pattern of church life. There are many of these. There are many cases of Churches of differing denominations co-operating in the work of the parish and in worship. In some places, especially in developing areas where new buildings have to be erected, the place of worship may be fully shared. Where the Church co-operates in community development, as in the examples mentioned earlier, a new pattern of life should begin to emerge. But elsewhere ecumenical action has often to be based on activities acceptable to those of various traditions and therefore tends to be cautious and conservative. But at least they give congregations the chance to look at their situation afresh.

Thirdly there are the activities that lead members of the congregation to go outside the Church and get into the world. The motive of these activities is, in the first instance, protest or compassion: the desire to do something about some local difficulty or national problem and the call to relieve suffering in some disaster. So action is apt to be limited to signing petitions and gathering money. It is as people begin to get involved in doing something themselves with other people that their political education begins and what is done outside the Church is seen as important. If this gathers force it means that church-members have less time to spend in the Church because they are engaged in the affairs of the world outside. It is impossible to decide how far this is happening. But there is no doubt that it is happening in many places. It is more doubtful whether the Church always welcomes it. For the more it happens the less does the congregation appear to be doing. But this is all to the good. It places action where action should be—in the work of members in the world.

The question we have to face is: how far are these

manifold but small changes in the life of the local church likely to effect a radical change in the over-all pattern of its life in the future? And what can the Church itself do to encourage such a change?

There have been attempts by the authorities of the Church to encourage and even to quicken change. There have also been changes in the administration of the Churches but these have not significantly affected the way the members live. Of the more or less official attempts to change the life of the Church we can mention three.

First of all there has been the setting up of special agencies to make experiments in particular areas. The most famous of these has been the East Harlem Protestant Parish in New York. This has been typical, as it has indeed been the inspirer, of many, usually smaller, enterprises to meet the needs of immigrant or underprivileged communities in cities in America and elsewhere. It has been as radical in its methods as many of the smaller experiments we have already mentioned. It has exhibited openness and a non-directive approach. It has accepted people as persons and offered them the means of finding their own way. It has depended on its staff living devoted and sacrificial lives together. But, unlike the other more private experiments, it has worked in the name of the Church with the aim of being the Church in its area. Their leaders have insisted that they are not dealing with a uniquely peculiar situation but prophetically with what would soon be the situation of the Church everywhere. On the whole the Church has regarded this work as an admirable piece of foreign missionary work carried out not overseas but, unfortunately, at home.

Because of the failure of such schemes to influence the life of the Church, attention has shifted, in America but also in Britain, to the training of the clergy for the service of the Church in this strange new world. An example is the

Urban Training Centre of Chicago. It has produced a lengthy scheme for the training of the clergy not in the study only but in the life of the city, especially the depressed inner city. This produces a new type of minister who is more likely to find his place in social service than back in a congregation. Would it not be better for the Church to inspire and help to train lay people for this work? What is the point of bringing in the idea of the ordained ministry unless the changes in their education are related to changes in the life and the thinking of the whole Church? It is the clergy that is being trained and not the Church. Is the Church as it is beyond need or beyond hope? As two who have studied the work write: 'For the most part, the structures of religion as they exist are accepted in outline.'[1] Most denominations face a serious drift of their clergy from the parish ministry. Men want to find a more demanding and more satisfying job. The basic problem is to change the life of the local church and this means the laity.

The years since the last war have seen a new interest in the education of the laity. And here we can speak of Europe rather than of America. In Britain, in addition to the centres mentioned in Chapter 3, there has been a proliferation of conference centres, retreat houses and organisations for the education of the laity. They serve the Church locally or nationally by helping its members to understand the world of the present and to prepare to serve the Church of the future. Compared with the American schemes of clerical training they are small and move forward slowly and cautiously. But this is of the nature of the laity. Lay people cannot be directed or organised or offered a job. They have in the end to be self-directed. So the schemes are held back by the people they are trying to lead forward. When they do take a step forward it is on their own.

[1] *Can These Bones Live?* p. 138

The German Church can display enterprises of lay education which make the British efforts seem puny, as the Evangelical Academies and the Kirkentag. These immense achievements represent the response of a nation and a Church to the need to rebuild a nation shattered by war and a Church that had lost its way. The aim of the academies was to build up an informed democracy by helping men to face the problems of their business and professional lives. The Kirkentag aimed to create a new sense of national unity on the basis of a Christian democracy. The achievements of both have been remarkable, though their task is unending. But it would be hazardous to suggest that any corresponding change has been conspicuous in the life of the local church.

One question remains unanswered. Can these experiments—of special mission, of clergy training, of laity education—help the local churches to find a new and fuller way of life? Or do they have the opposite effect? Do they draw off those who might have become pioneers and innovators and leave the churches in the hands of the conservative and timid? Have the experimenters given up the Church as they know it as hopeless? If they have, should they not be trying to follow up their experiments with a deliberate attempt to build an alternative Church, for all their experiments assume that there must be some kind of continuing organisation? Will it take an economic catastrophe to waken us up, too late?

It is impossible to forecast what might happen to enable the Church to throw off its rigidity of mind and action. We are saying the same thing if we ask how can the Church learn to respond to God's moving Spirit, which blows in the world before it is felt in the Church.

But three things would seem to be needed. And they are in the hands of the Church as it is.

The first thing that is needed is the recognition of

change: not the timid realisation that unfortunately things are not the same as they once were, but the joyful recognition that change is the condition of life. It is something we know all through our individual lives. We have to learn to live in the strange world into which we are born. We have to learn how to survive and how to live with other people. We pass from being a child to being a parent without much training or any experience. We face new situations and new problems all the time. It is the same with the Church. The pattern of the past can never fit the present. There is nothing sacrosanct about anything we do in church buildings. The congregation that we take for granted is only a passing form, no more the pattern for the future than it was for the past. The shaking up of our thinking and of our expectations depends on the nature of our faith. Do we believe in an institution or in the Spirit? Do we look to the future or to the past? These are questions we must answer for ourselves. No one else can answer them for us.

Secondly, life does not come down to us from the top. It is no use waiting for the powers that be in the Church to solve our problems for us. Christians have to take their freedom and assert their responsibility. It is in the grass that the wind of the Spirit is felt, not in the clear sky or the racing clouds. But the structure of authority in any church can defy the movement of the Spirit and stop things from happening. It can impose a pattern on a mesmerised people. It certainly decides the agenda of church meetings. It was fashionable a few years ago to say that the world sets the agenda of the Church. If this meant that the world decides and the Church follows, the saying has a cynical truth. But it was used to suggest that the Church should be much more concerned with the affairs of the world. And the courts of the Church now give more time to the discussion of social, economic and political questions. But 'agenda' means doing not discussing. The agenda of the

Church—the matters on which it acts—have still to do with ecclesiastical affairs—with its property, the recruiting and pay of its staff and the administration of its business. On these matters it does not just pass a resolution; it acts. And this idea of acting only on its own affairs goes right down to the affairs of the local church. The members of the Church have been trained to think that all that matters is to keep the institution going. The authorities of the Church could release the whole Church from this bondage, by altering their own agenda. Perhaps they alone can do it. But will they?

The third thing that is within the power of the Church is the education of its members. Future ages may well look back with surprise and amazement at the millions that have been poured out last century and this on the education of the clergy and the failure to spend any money or to give any thought to the education of the laity. We are only beginning to realise what a waste of money and squandering of man-power it has been and what an opportunity was missed. The problem that now faces the Church is new and stupendous. It is essentially the question of adult education. It is our own education. It must be free and it knows no authority. It has to do with the living of our own lives, not other people's lives, and with the doing of our own jobs, not other people's jobs. But it is not an individual thing. For we live with other people and we work with other people. No one can do it for us. And no one can make us do it. The only possible consolation for the Church's failure in the past is that if instead of educating the clergy it had educated the laity it would have done the right job in the wrong way. Perhaps we can begin now with a freedom and flexibility unknown before. But we shall have to shake ourselves free of the domination of the past and the dogmatism of the clergy. But this is up to the Church. Experiments can point the way but only the members of the Church can do anything about following it.

The Church as it is has far greater power and opportunities than it sometimes imagines.

9 *The moving spirit*

THE WORD 'EXPERIMENT' has intruded into this book more than was intended. It's an awkward word. It is associated with scientific investigation. It's taken to mean trying out something for the first time or to gather more facts. This is not the sense in which it has been used here. Most of the activities of which we have been thinking have been undertaken by people who, indeed, know that they were doing them for the first time, at least so far as they were concerned. But this was not their reason for doing them. They were not out to prove anything or to test a theory, though undoubtedly they hoped to discover things in the bygoing. They did what they did because this was the thing they wanted to do, this was the life they had to live. We have called their actions experiments for lack of a better word. Sometimes for the sake of variety we have referred to them as enterprises. But this word is a bit ponderous. It gives no hint of the venture which their activities express.

This willingness to do things for the first time and with other people, just because you want to do them, is basic to the Christian faith. The greatest experiment in the world was made by Jesus in the life he lived. He was not trying to prove anything. He was not following a line to see what would happen. He was not wanting to see if his ideas would work. He knew that in the eyes of the world they would not work. He knew that he would be killed. But he knew that what he did he had to do because it was the one thing that he wanted to do.

When we talk about the Spirit, isn't this what we mean? We see in Jesus' life the supreme manifestation of the power of the Spirit. This is what it means to talk about the creative spirit by which all things exist and men are alive. Man's awareness of this is what marks him as made in the image of God. His awareness of the Spirit as his is seen in his willingness to respond to what he finds in life and his intention to do things on his own. This does not, of course, mean that his judgement of what to do is always sound or the things he does are always right.

We can say more about the Spirit from our understanding of Jesus and of ourselves. We know that it brings people together: that we cannot think about the Spirit without talking about the fellowship of the Spirit. And being with others leads us into action. And this means continuity. The Spirit is spontaneous but it is not sporadic. It is immediate and it is enduring.

The marks of the Spirit are that it initiates, it is corporate and it endures. These are the signs of its presence that should always be evident in the Church. And it is along these lines alone that we can dare to talk about the pattern of the life of the Church in the future. It is easy enough to draw a picture of what we think the Church of the future should be like. It is even easier to draw a caricature of what we fear the Church may well be like. Both are unprofitable tasks. The one thing certain is that the Church of the future will be like neither. Events and the Spirit will see to this.

But the essential importance of these three marks is unavoidable. They belong to the nature of life; both what we call natural life and what we call transcendant life. If they are suppressed in the Church by convention, fear or pride, they will appear elsewhere in the structures that men build in order to love. For men have always to find new ways to respond to what is happening. And men have to find ways of living together wherever they are. They have to maintain life for their children and for those who follow them. The events of our time make this the more urgent. We have today to do things for the efficient doing of which the experience of previous generations can give us little help. We have to live with those with whom previous generations had no personal dealings. Whether we like it or not, we are one large family on earth living in too small a house. We have to learn to live together. We have to safeguard the world for the future. Most of the things we need to do we do for the first time. We have to trust the Spirit.

The Church claims to know the Spirit. It claims personally to know the Spirit by whom all men live. This surely means that the marks of the Spirit have to enliven the life of the Church now in a revolutionary way to bring hope to men. It is this that links together the scattered experiments and the on-going life of the Church.

Most people in the Church would have no doubt about the value of endurance or continuity or tradition or however they like to call the sense of being committed to a gospel that is of old and for ever. They would probably also agree that the essential nature of the Church is corporate. But many would question the need for experiment. Some would feel it treason to tradition. Others might say that probably they had got set in their ways and that for the sake of keeping the younger people the Church should try new ways. A few might say that only experiments will save the situation now: anything so long as it is new.

All these attitudes deny the Spirit. Can the Church welcome change for itself, not because change is forced on it, or because it is worried about money and numbers, but because it believes that in Christ all things are made new. The Church in the future will certainly find that its way of life is being changed. But will it be glad that it cannot go on as before? Any idea of uniformity will have to go. This is what all the experiments are saying. The Church can no longer be made up of a vast number of local congregations all attempting to do exactly the same thing. Inevitably there are going to be in the future a great many groups of all kinds, with different interests and doing different things and quite unrelated. They will be composed of all sorts of people, with diverse ideas, opinions and attitudes but all regarded equally as the Church. This spells the end of uniformity, both in organisation and in belief. Orthodoxy becomes meaningless. Unity will have to be sought elsewhere than in structure or creed. Indeed the task of the Church will be to find a new unity for all men. The Church will have no doubt that it is to be found in Jesus: not in a statement of belief about Jesus but in his visible or hidden life among men.

This dangerous readiness to find new ways is the first demand that the Spirit makes on the Church today.

The second concerns fellowship. The fellowship that the Church—and the world—are being led into is fellowship with all men and not just with other members of the Church. This is not distant, theoretical prospect. We live our lives now with all other men. The Church has to find how it lives its life with them. It does not do so by shutting doors and keeping people out. It does not do so by tests of belief or behaviour. It cannot do so by the crusade that attacks or by the mission that woos. Once you share people's lives you can no longer be on the offensive or on the defensive. How does the Church change to this kind of way of living?

And the Church goes on and will go on. But the endurance demanded is not the defence of entrenched positions. It is the endurance that is willing to be on the move into a new freedom of openness and experiment.

What else can it mean to talk of God's moving spirit?

Some useful books

CHAPTER 1

Peoples's Church; a Directory of Christian Alternatives
SCM pamphlet: a list of some 220 alternatives in Britain, with a brief description in some cases. Questions arise as to why some are in and others are not.

CHAPTER 2

Religion and Change by David L. Edwards; Hodder and Stoughton, 1969.

The Church, Change and Development by Ivan Illich; Urban Training Centre Press; Herder and Herder, 1970.

CHAPTER 3

Signs of Renewal edited by Hans-Ruedi Eber; World Council of Churches, 1956.

Living Springs: New Religious Movements in Western Europe by Olive Wyon; SCM Press, 1963.

On Taize:

Tomorrow is Too Late: Taize an experiment in Christian Community by Peter C. Moore; A. R. Mowbray, 1970.

The Rule of Taize by Roger Schutz.

Taize; Le concile des Jeunes, monthly.

On Iona:

We Shall Rebuild by George F. MacLeod; The Iona Community, 1945.

100   God's moving spirit

Only One Way Left by George F. MacLeod; The Iona
    Community, 1956.
What is the Iona Community? by T. Ralph Morton; the
    Iona Community, 1969.

On the Kirkentag:
*A Man to be Reckoned with: The Story of Reinold von
    Thadden-Trieglaff* by Werner Huhne, edited by Mark
    Gibbs; SCM Press, 1962.

CHAPTER 4
Community a periodical published under the auspices of
    'One for Christian renewal' (c/o Publishing Services
    Partnership, 82 High Road, London, N2 9PW).
Communes USA: A Personal Tour by Richard Fairfield;
    Penguin Books Inc. Baltimore, 1972.
The Joyful Community: An account of the Bruderhof by
    Benjamin Zablocki; Penguin Books Inc. Baltimore,
    1971.

CHAPTER 5
On Industrial Mission:
The Christian Witness in an Industrial Society by Horst
    Symanowski; Collins.
God on Monday by Simon Phipps; Hodder and Stoughton,
    1966.
On-the-job Ethics edited by Cameron P. Hall; National
    Council of Churches in the USA, 1963.

On industrial experiments:
*Sharing our Industrial Future; a study of employee par-
    ticipation* by Roger Sawtell; The Industrial Society,
    1968.
The papers of *The Industrial Common-Ownership Move-
    ment* (The Secretary, 8 Churton Street, London,
    SW1.)

On Community Development:

The Non-Directive Approach in Group and Community Work by T. R. Batten; Oxford University Press, 1967.

The Church and Community Development: an Introduction by George Lovell; Grail Publications/Chester House Publications, 1972.

Parchmore Occasional Papers, Parchmore Church Youth and Community Centre, 55 Parchmore Road, Thornton Heath, Surrey. The address of The Church and Community Development Project 70–75 is 125 Waxwell Lane, Pinner, Middlesex, HA5 3ER.

CHAPTER 6

A general survey of the contemporary American scene:

Can These Bones Live? The Failure of Church Renewal by Robert S. Lecky and H. Elliott Wright; Sheed and Ward, New York; 1969.

On Pentecostalism:

The Pentecostals by Walter J. Hollenweger; SCM Press, 1972.

Nine O'Clock in the Morning by Dennis J. Bennett; Coverdale House Publishers, London and Eastbourne, 1971.

On the Church of the Saviour:

Call to Commitment; the Story of the Church of the Saviour by Elizabeth O'Connor; Harper and Row, 1963.

Journey Inward, Journey Outward by Elizabeth O'Connor, Harper and Row, 1968.

On the Underground Church:

America is Hard to Find by Daniel Berrigan; SPCK, London; 1973.

The Underground Church edited by Malcolm Boyd; Sheed and Ward, 1969.

On the 'Jesus Movement':
Pop goes Jesus by Micheal Jacob; Mowbrays, 1972.
The Jesus Kids by Roger C. Palms; SCM Press, 1972.

CHAPTER 7

Naturally there is no book specifically on this subject. Two point to the background:

God outside the Church by J. W. Stevenson; Saint Andrew Press, Edinburgh, 1972.

Mankind my Church by Colin Morris; Hodder and Stoughton, 1971.

CHAPTER 8

Experiments in Renewal edited by Anthony J. Wesson; Epworth Press, 1971.

Case Studies in Unity by R. M. C. Jeffery; SCM press, 1972.

Churches on the Move by Gunnel Vallquist; Fortress Press, Philadelphia, 1970.

First the Political Kingdom by Brian Wicker; Sheed and Ward, 1967.

God's Colony in Man's World by George W. Webber; Abington Press, 1960.

The Congregation in Mission by George W. Webber, Abingdon Press, 1964.